George Pliny Brown, Ruth Morris

A Course of Composition and Grammar for the Primary and Grammar Grades of the Indianapolis Public Schools

George Pliny Brown, Ruth Morris

A Course of Composition and Grammar for the Primary and Grammar Grades of the Indianapolis Public Schools

ISBN/EAN: 9783337294052

Printed in Europe, USA, Canada, Australia, Japan

Cover: Foto ©Paul-Georg Meister /pixelio.de

More available books at **www.hansebooks.com**

A COURSE

IN

COMPOSITION AND GRAMMAR

FOR THE

PRIMARY AND GRAMMAR GRADES

OF THE

INDIANAPOLIS PUBLIC SCHOOLS.

PREPARED BY
GEO. P. BROWN AND RUTH MORRIS.

INDIANAPOLIS:
1877.

Entered according to Act of Congress, in the year 1877, by

GEORGE P. BROWN
and
RUTH MORRIS,

In the Office of Librarian of Congress at Washington.

PREFACE.

The following Manual presents an outline of the course in Composition actually pursued in the Primary and Grammar departments of the Public Schools of Indianapolis, together with a detailed statement of the course in Grammar for the three upper grades.

In the first five grades, Grammar and Composition are taught together. Grammatical forms are learned as they are used in expressing thought. At the beginning of the sixth year the study of the sentence as a whole, and in its parts, is begun. This is a work so different from that of Composition, that the two subjects are taught separately for the next three years. Three recitations are required each week in Grammar, and two in Composition.

An outline of the course in Grammar for the Sixth Grade will be found in Chapter VI. of the Course in Composition, Part II.

Pupils in the Seventh Grade complete the first twelve chapters of "Lessons in Grammar." These are reviewed in the Eighth Grade, and the remainder of Part I. is completed.

In the preparation of the "Lessons in Grammar," an effort has been made to lead the pupils to see that the forms and uses of words are determined by the thought to be expressed. A classification of attributes and of objects,—the material with which the mind deals in forming thoughts,—and the separation of the thought into its elements, prepares the pupil to comprehend more fully the office of the sentence in expressing this thought. Starting with the sentence as the unit of language, he learns by the processes of analysis and synthesis, the use of words, phrases, and clauses, in giving expression to an unlimited number and variety of thoughts. He is next led to see that this large amount of material out of which sentences are constructed, can all be separated into seven distinct classes or groups; viz., (1) those words that denote objects of thought,—*nouns* and *pronouns;* (2) those words that denote attributes of objects,—*adjectives ;*

(3) those words that denote attributes of attributes,—*adverbs;* (4) those words that denote the judging act of the mind,—*verbs;* (5) those words that express relations of objects and attributes,—*prepositions;* (6) those words that express relations of thoughts,—*conjunctions;* (7) those words that express feeling,—*interjections.*

After a brief study of each of these classes, and of the principal sub-classes under each, the pupil is prepared to see that the inflection of words is but another way of denoting a change in their meaning: that instead of using words, phrases, and clauses, changes in the form of the word itself are introduced, to denote certain modifications of the thought.

This Manual is full of errors, some of which may be charged to the printer, but the authors are conscious that the most serious faults are chargeable to them. Their apology is, that the different chapters have been written at such times as could be taken from other duties, and no time has been found for revision or correction.

LESSONS IN GRAMMAR.

CHAPTER I.

ATTRIBUTES.

The sun may be known and distinguished from other objects by its *brightness*, its *warmth*, its *roundness*, etc.; a slate, by being *hard, opaque*, etc.; an apple, by being *ripe* or *unripe, large* or *small, red, green*, etc.

Brightness, warmth, hardness, ripeness, etc., are called attributes of the objects to which they belong.

An Attribute is that by which an object is known or distinguished.

Of the attributes mentioned above, brightness, warmth, roundness, and hardness are permanent attributes of their objects. They can not change unless the nature of the object changes. An object that was not bright, warm, and round would not be the sun, but some different object. Such attributes are called *qualities*.

A Quality is an attribute that is viewed as belonging to its object permanently.

When we think of the sky as cloudy, the weather as rainy, the apple as hard or mellow, we do not regard these attributes as permanent, enduring so long as the object exists; but as *states* or *conditions* of the objects. We can think of them as ceasing or changing, without any such change in the nature of the object as to make it a different object from what it was before. Such attributes are called *attributes of condition*.

An Attribute of Condition is an attribute that is viewed as belonging to its object only for a time, and may change without a change in the nature of the object.

Exercise.

Distinguish the words in the following that express attributes of quality, from those expressing attributes of condition:

Cold winter. Frosty weather. Round earth. White snow. Cloudy sky. Shining sun. The old man. Green grass. The hungry dog. The rising sun. The new moon. Balmy spring. An open window. Bright days. Sour apples. Black cloth. Skillful artisans. Soaring eagles. Working bees.

Model.—A red flower. A faded flower. The word red expresses a quality. The word faded expresses a condition.

Give five original illustrations of attributes of quality; five of attributes of condition.

John studies. My horse runs. Those swallows fly. Here the subjects are known by certain actions they perform. These actions are therefore attributes.

An Attribute of Action is one that represents an object as acting.

In the sentence, "The apple is larger than the peach," we distinguish the apple by stating the relation that it bears to the peach in respect of size. When we say "The rose is more fragrant than the lily," we have distinguished the rose by stating the relation it bears to the lily in respect of odor.

"A large house stands on the hill." Here, by the use of the word *large*, we imply that there is something else with which the house is compared. It is either compared with other houses of its own class, or with other houses in general, or with the use commonly made of houses; and the conclusion is reached that this particular house is large. If the house be a dwelling house, it may be large when compared with other dwelling houses, but when compared with a church or a court-house it is small. Or if it is large when compared with other houses in general, yet when compared with a mountain it is small.

Thus we see that objects may be known or distinguished by certain relations that they bear to other objects. These relations are, therefore, attributes.

An Attribute of Relation is an attribute that distinguishes its object by referring in some way to some other object.

The relation between objects may be in respect of color, odor, size, form, weight, etc.; or it may be that of cause and effect; as, the rain *moistens* the earth; sunshine *ripens* the fruit; or it may be that of action; as, John *outran* James. The different classes of relations that may exist between objects are very numerous.

In the sentence, "James is here," the word, *here*, shows where James is; or, stated differently, it shows his relation to space. So in the sentence, "The pencil is in my hand," the words, *in my hand*, show the place of the pencil,—where it is located in space.

In the sentence, "The meeting was yesterday," the word, *yesterday*, tells when the meeting was; it expresses the time of the meeting. Hence we say that it shows the relation of the meeting to time.

Attributes of relation may be of three classes: (1) those that show the relation of the object to space; (2) those that show the relation of the object to time; (3) those that show the relation of one object to another.

We have found that there are four classes of attributes; viz., Qualities, Actions, Conditions and Relations.

Exercise.

Classify the attributes expressed in the following: Chalk is brittle. Fishes swim. Glass is transparent. My brother is sick. The courthouse is on Washington street. The child is asleep. The street is muddy. The eclipse was yesterday. You are in haste. Rubber is elastic. Frost benefits the soil. The blue sky is overhead. The grass is parched and dry.

John is more industrious than his brother. The workmen built the house. Paint improves houses. The elm is more symmetrical than the ash. Common air outweighs smoke. The weather is cold and rainy. The ship is in decay. Aloes are bitter. The old man is here. John is the tallest man in town. Life is sometimes bright and fair, and sometimes dark and lonely. Severe exercise in summer is exhausting.

Write five original sentences, illustrating attributes of quality; of condition; of action; of relation. State the kind of relation expressed in each. State the difference between the attributes of quality and those of condition.

NOTE.—The *attributes* of objects should be carefully distinguished from the *parts* of objects.

CHAPTER II.

OBJECTS.

Abstracts, Concretes.

The object to which an attribute belongs, is the *subject* of the attribute.

Exercise.

Name, in the following, the words expressing attributes, and those expressing the subjects of these attributes:

James is studious. Frank grows. Doves coo. The weather is warm. The old man is here. The brave soldiers fought. The busy bee gathers honey. The lecture was on Friday. My new book is on the table. Tall, graceful pillars support the roof.

The attributes expressed in the preceding exercises are all viewed as connected with their subjects. This is the original and natural way of viewing attributes. The color green, for example, is first known as connected with and belonging to the grass, the leaves, or to some other object. It is possible, however, for us to think of the color green, without connecting it with any particular object. We thus abstract it from all objects and think only of the attribute itself; as when we say, "Greenness is a color belonging to many objects."

When thus separated or *abstracted* from all objects, the attribute itself is viewed as an object. It has no real existence apart from some object, but we think of it and talk of it as if it had.

An attribute thought apart from its subject is called an *abstract object*, or an *abstract*.

The form of the word expressing an *abstract* is usually different from that which expresses the attribute proper: Examples.—The word "hard" expresses an attribute proper, "hardness," an abstact; "beautiful" expresses an attribute proper, "beauty," an abstract; "timid," an attribute; "timidity," an abstract.

NOTE.—Words expressing *abstracts* end in "ness," "ty," "th," "nce," "tion," "sion," "ing," "age," "ment," "ure," etc.

Exercise.

State which of the following words express abstracts, and which, attributes proper:—White; whiteness; soft; heavy; smoothness; quickness; large; solidity; humid; honesty; true; truth; color.

Since there are four classes of attributes, there must be four classes of *abstracts*: viz., Abstracts (1) of quality, (2) of action, (3) of condition, (4) of relation.

Exercise.

Name and designate the classes of *abstracts* expressed in the following:

Change all the words expressing abstracts to forms that will express attributes proper.

The brightness of the sun is dazzling. Fragrance belongs to the rose. The sickness of his brother detained him. Running is tiresome. Resistance is useless. The tartness of the apple is unpleasant. By exercise we gain strength. The excessive heat of the summer was depressing. The superiority of his brother was manifest. Gravity and dignity are becoming. The remoteness of the country made communication difficult. Patience and perseverance remove mountains. Surely goodness and mercy shall follow me.

Write five original sentences, in which abstracts of quality are expressed; five, of condition; five, of action; five, of relation.

Both abstract objects and attributes proper may have attributes.

Examples:—Singing *pleases*. Modesty is *attractive*. *Kind* actions *promote* happiness. The orator speaks *fluently*. The white snow falls *softly* and *silently*. The words, "pleases," "attractive," "kind," and "promote" express attributes of abstracts. "Fluently," "softly," and "silently" express attributes of other attributes.

Write five original sentences, expressing in each an attribute of an attribute; five, expressing an attribute of an abstract. Designate.

Select sentences from the reader illustrating the same. Name the attribute in each case.

There is another class of objects that are real objects. A horse, a man, the sun, a house, the mind, are not first known as attributes of other objects, as abstracts are, but they are known only as subjects of attributes. Such objects are called *concrete objects* or *concretes*.

A Concrete is an object only known as a subject having attributes:

Or,

Objects that are not known as attributes, are **Concretes.**

Exercise.

Point out in the following sentence, (1) all words expressing *concretes;* (2) all those expressing *abstracts;* (3) all those expressing attributes of *concretes*, or of *abstracts;* (4) all expressing attributes of *attributes.*

Name the class to which each attribute belongs.

The house is new. Charity is kind. Forbearance is praiseworthy. Rain fell last night. The children are poor, hungry, cold, and friendless. Wisdom is better than gold. Truth and candor possess a powerful charm. White clouds float along the sky softly and tranquilly. Virtue attendeth at her right hand. Down the smooth rock, melodious waters glide.

They softly lie and sweetly sleep,
Low in the ground.

Attributes, { Quality. Condition. Action. Relation. }   Objects, { Concrete. Abstract. }

¶ State the resemblances and differences between Concretes, Abstracts, and Attributes.

CHAPTER III.

A THOUGHT OR JUDGMENT.

When we think something of some object, a thought or judgment is formed.

Examples: The apple is sweet. Snow is white. The pencil is hard.

When we analyze the first example, we find that there are three elements to be considered: (1) *that of which we think;* viz., the apple: (2) *that which we think of the apple;* viz., sweet: (3) *the relation that the mind discerns as existing between these,* expressed by " is." The first and second elements constitute the matter of thought. They are the material with which the mind deals; but there is no thought formed, until the mind discerns that sweetness is an attribute belonging to the apple : that is, until it discerns the relation existing between the first two elements.

NOTE.—This relation is different in different thoughts. In the example, "Grant is President," that of which we think,—Grant,—and that which we think of this object,—the president,—are represented as being one and the same person. There is no difference between the president, and Grant; they are totally indentical. The relation discerned between these two elements is that of *total identity*.

In the example, "The snow is white," whiteness is thought to be identical with one attribute of snow only; it is only partially the same as snow. The relation is, therefore, one of *partial identity*.

In the example, "Chalk is not black," we think that there is no attribute of chalk that is the same as blackness. Hence we say that the relation discerned between chalk and black is one of *non-identity*.

In every thought, some one of these relations must be discerned.

The three elements of the thought are named *the subject, the predicate,* and *the copula.*

The Subject of the Thought is that of which something is thought.

The Predicate of the Thought is that which is thought of the subject.

The Copula of the Thought is the relation between the subject and predicate, as discerned by the mind.

NOTE TO TEACHERS.—In this discussion, the thought has been viewed as a product. It is possible to view it as a process; in which case the copula would be defined to be the *thinking* or *judging act* of the mind.

CHAPTER IV.

THE SENTENCE.

There are many ways of expressing thoughts: e. g., by signs and gestures, by inarticulate sounds, by pictures, by objects. In fact, everything that exists is an expression of thought. The house that we live in, the clothes that we wear, the food that we eat, the flowers, the grass, the trees, the stars, all express thoughts. Among rational beings, the commonest way of expressing thoughts is by the use of words.

A group of words expressing a thought is a **Sentence.**

Exercise.

State which words in the following sentences express subjects of thought; which express predicates; which express copulas. State whether the subject and predicate are identical or non-identical, and whether the identity is total or partial:

The knife is new. John is not studious. The earth is round. Two and two are four. The man is an artist. James is erect. •Slate is transparent. The ship was the Pacific. Iron is a mineral. A tree is root, trunk, branches, and leaves. Truth is virtue. A triangle is a three-sided figure. Leaves are green. Austin was the governor. John is a post-master. Birds are fowls.

Since the subject, predicate, and copula are each essential to the existence of a thought, they are called the *elements* of a thought.

Since the thought has three elements, the sentence which expresses the thought has three elements, called *subject, predicate,* and *copula.*

The Subject of a Sentence is that element which expresses the subject of the thought.

The Predicate of a Sentence is that element which expresses the predicate of thought.

The Copula of a Sentence is that element which expresses the copula of the thought:

Or,

The Copula of a Sentence is that element which expresses the relation discerned between the subject and predicate of thought.

Exercise.

Point out the *subjects, predicates,* and *copulas,* in the following sentences:

Water is tasteless. Fawns are timid. Dogs are quadrupeds. Man is mortal. Diamonds are combustible. Stars are suns. Vinegar is sour. Snow is not black.

What relation exists between the subject of thought and the subject of the sentence? What, between the subject of thought and the subject of an attribute?

The copula and the predicate in each of the sentences in the preceding exercise are separate words. In the sentences, "Flowers bloom," "Ice melts," "Birds twitter," and the like, they are united in one word.

Write five original sentences in which each element consists of a single word; five, in which the predicate and copula are united in one word.

Select from the reader ten sentences of each class.

Predicates may express concrete or abstract objects, or they may express attributes of these objects.

Examples:—Trees are *plants*. (concrete.) Patience is a *virtue*. (abstract.) Washington was *brave*. (attribute of concrete.) Cowardice is *disgraceful*. (attribute of abstract.)

A predicate that expresses an attribute, is an *attributive predicate*.

Predicates that express concrete or abstract objects, are *non-attributive predicates*.

Exercise.

Write ten original sentences containing attributive predicates: ten, containing non-attributive predicates.

Classify the predicates in the following sentences:

Grass grows. Knowledge is powerful. Knowledge is power. Dogs are animals. The mind thinks. The sun is in the heavens. The sea is at rest. The lightning flashes. The apple is mellow. John is a good boy. The dead leaves fall. The tree is a poplar. Pure water is tasteless. Vulcan was a blacksmith. Morning dawns. Mary is superior to her classmates.

NOTE.—When the copula and predicate are united in one word, the predicate is always attributive.

CHAPTER V.

MODIFIERS.

In the sentence, "Man is mortal," all human beings are included. The application of the word *man* is not limited to an individual, nor to a class of men. In the sentence, "That tall man is a soldier," the word man applies to only one individual. This change in the application of the word, is produced by the words *that* and *tall*. They limit the meaning to one particular man. If we say, "Man is a soldier," we include all men. By the addition of the word *tall*, we exclude all except tall men, but we include all *tall* men. We limit the application of the word to a class. But when we say, "*That* tall man," we limit the application to a single one of the class.

Words used to *limit the application* of other words are called *modifying words*.

"Sparkling diamonds," "Silent flowers."—The words *sparkling* and *silent* are not here used to limit the application of the words to which they are added. All diamonds are sparkling and all flowers are silent. They are used to call attention to, and make more prominent, qualities that belong to all diamonds and all flowers. Such words are also called modifying words.

The office of all modifying words,—whether they limit the application, or give prominence to an attribute,—is to make the meaning of the words to which they are added, more definite.

A Modifying Word is a word added to another word to make its meaning more definite.

Exercise.

Point out the modifying words in the following, and distinguish those limiting the application of other words, from those used to give prominence to some attribute:—Red apples. Twinkling stars. Revolving planets. Pleasant faces. Bristling spears. Old men. Purple flowers. Checkered life. Tall girls. Kind hearts. Unfading hope. Starless despair. Golden clouds. Ruffled spirits. Green emeralds. A wild, woody dingle.

That part of the subject, predicate, or copula, to which modifying words are added, is the *principal part*.

That part of each element consisting of one or more modifying words, is the *modifying part*.

The predicate and copula, whether combined or uncombined, may contain a principal and a modifying part.

Examples.—John is *probably very* studious. John *probably* studies *very* hard.

In the first sentence the copula and predicate are uncombined and each contains a modifier. In the second example, the predicate and copula are united in one word and each element contains a modifier. As predicate, the word "studies" is modified by the word "hard;" as copula, by the word "probably."

NOTE:—The sentence, "John is studious," shows that we think the attribute expressed in the word ' studious," of John. But when we say, "John is probably studious," it shows that we are in some doubt as to whether John is studious or not. The relation between John and this attribute is expressed as uncertain or doubtful. But when we say, "John is *certainly* studious," we make it very emphatic that we think the attribute expressed in the word "studious" belongs to John. We see that both "probably" and "certainly" refer to the relation discerned between the subject and the predicate of thought: therefore they belong to the copula of the sentence.

Exercise.

Write five sentences in which the predicate and copula are combined, and each element contains a modifying word; five, in which they are uncombined and each element contains a modifying part; five, in which all the elements contain modifying words.

The principal part of the subject, predicate, or copula, is called the *grammatical* subject, predicate, or copula.

When there are no modifying words, the grammatical and logical elements are the same.

Exercise.

Separate each of the following sentences into its logical and grammatical elements:

State whether the predicate and copula are combined or uncombined, and whether the predicate is attributive or non-attributive.

Mary writes. Gold is valuable. He is brave. You are indeed kind. No fearful plague raged there. The north wind blows violently to-night. He necessarily remains weak. He finally started. The standard was probably low. Undoubtedly he is a great man. The large hall was brilliantly illuminated. These, perhaps, are foolish feelings. A crimson rose is certainly a beautiful flower.

The principal part of an attributive predicate may be modified by a word expressing an attribute; as, Mary thinks *accurately*. James works *well*. The sea is *beautifully* blue.

Such words are called *Attributive Modifiers*.

Write five sentences which shall contain attributive predicates having attributive modifiers.

Point out the attributive modifiers in the preceding exercise.

In the sentence, "Cain slew Abel," the principal part of the predicate is modified by the word "Abel," which expresses the immediate object of the action expressed in in the word "slew." In the sentence, "John outran James," a relation is expressed having James as the direct object. In the sentence, "He gave the book to me," the principal part of the predicate is modified by the words "book" and "me." The word "book" expresses the direct object of the action expressed in the word "gave," and the word "me" the indirect or remote object.

A modifying word that expresses the object of an action or relation, is called an **Objective Modifier.**

An objective modifier that expresses the immediate object of an action or relation, is a *direct objective modifier.* One that expresses a remote object, is an *indirect objective modifier.*

Exercise.

Define an attributive modifier; an objective modifier; a direct objective modifier; an indirect objective modifier.

Write sentences illustrating the use of these different classes of modifiers.

Point out the attributive and the objective modifiers in the following, and distinguish the direct from the indirect objective modifiers:

The rain falls softly. The cattle eat grass. The clouds are wonderfully beautiful. The boy broke the window. The great ship moves slowly. Grace lost the ball. The water is very deep. William conquered England. I am too idle. The sun fades the carpet. He went to New York. He saw the general. He was lately here. The smoke descends slowly. The party visited the falls. John spoke of his father. Do me the favor. A soft answer turneth away wrath. She wrote a letter to her sister. Sunlight falls on the castle walls. They stopped where night overtook them. I work for my uncle. Provide the stranger food. Deliver us from evil. Tell me the story.

When we say, "Victoria, the queen," "Milton, the poet," "Hendricks, the governor,"—we use the words "queen," "poet," and "governor," to show more clearly to whom the names "Victoria,"

"Milton" and "Hendricks," apply; i. e., to explain or identify the meaning of these words.

Such words are called *appositive modifiers* or *appositives.*

Define an appositive.

Write five sentences with appositive modifiers in the subject; five, with appositive modifiers in the predicate.

A modifier may be two or more words connected in meaning. If these words are so connected as to express a thought they form a *Clause.* If they are connected in meaning without expressing a thought they form a *Phrase.*

Examples.—Mary sings *very sweetly.* The *long expected* summer came. The tree *that fell* was an elm. I know *why they came.*

The words, *very sweetly* and *long expected,* are here used as *phrase* modifiers. The words *that fell,* and *why they came,* form *clause* modifiers.

Distinguish the phrase and the clause modifiers in the following:

The class solved a difficult problem. They heard Webster, the great orator. This is the lesson that I recited. James wrote a long letter to his aged father. Washington, the first president, served eight years. I know John is studious. A king who is just, helps the people. He is the man who rendered the service. John rides that wild horse. The place where he fell is unknown.

Select from your reader ten sentences containing phrase modifiers; and ten, containing clause modifiers.

Write five sentences in which phrase modifiers are used in the subject; five, in which clause modifiers are used in the predicate.

The copula may contain a phrase or a clause modifier.

Examples.—It is *without doubt* a fine picture. *If he had been here,* the accident would have been prevented.

Any element or part of an element of a sentence, that of itself expresses a thought, forms a clause.

Stated differently,—

A sentence that forms an element or a part of an element of another sentence, is a clause.

NOTE.—The principal part of an element of the sentence is sometimes a phrase or a clause.

Examples.—Mary is *in the room*. The statement is, *matter is indestructible*.

Why do we use modifying words?

CHAPTER VI.

PARTS OF SPEECH.

Nouns and Pronouns.

Concretes and Abstracts are either expressed by words which are names of these objects; as, *Henry, book, goodness;* or they are expressed by words which denote the objects without naming them; as, *I, thou, he, she, it, they, who, which, what, that.*

Words that are names of *concretes* and *abstracts* are called *Nouns*. Words that denote these objects without naming them are called *Pronouns*.

A Noun is a word that is the name of an object.

A Pronoun is a word that denotes an object without naming it.

Exercise.

Select the nouns and the pronouns in the following, and tell to what element of the sentence they belong:

We all consented. Columbus was a native of Genoa. He ran forward and kissed him. An unyielding firmness was displayed. While the bridegroom tarried they all slumbered and slept. He who will not be ruled by the rudder must be ruled by the mast. The deafening waves dash angrily. Charity begins at home, but it should not stay there.

>Dear little blossoms down under the snow,
>You must be weary of winter I know.

The subject of thought is always a concrete or an abstract object; hence a word that is the principal part of the subject of the sentence is always a noun or a pronoun.

The noun is used in other parts of the sentence, but since it names that of which something may be predicated, it is properly a subject-word.

Another definition of the noun is, *A word which is properly a subject word.*

Nouns that name concretes are called *concrete nouns;* those that name abstracts are called *abstract nouns.*

Exercise.

Point out the concrete and abstract nouns in the following:

The trees are in their fullest foliage. The multitude ran before him. Gloom filled every house. The bees make a perpetual murmur of delight. Each moment is a perfumed rose. Labor disgraces no man. Even the green trees partake the deep contentment. The woods are gay with the clustered flowers of the laurel. When the righteous are in authority, the people rejoice. Kindness of manner makes politeness. The acquisition of knowledge is one of the most pleasing employments of the human mind. Rivulets should send a voice of gladness from their winding paths.

"And the flakes of spray that were jerked away
From the froth on the lip of the bleak blue sea,
Were sometimes flung by the wind as it sung
Over turret, and terrace, and balcony."

NOTE.—Phrases and clauses may be used as nouns.

Examples.—*To err* is human. *To be idle* is wrong. *Why he went* is not known.

Adjectives.

Attributes of concretes and of abstracts are expressed by words that modify the meaning of the subject-word or noun; as, *Brave* men fell. He was a *brave* man. *White* lilies are beautiful.

They may also be expressed by words that are used as the principal part of the uncombined attributive predicate; as, The men are *brave.* The lilies are *white.*

Such words are called *Adjectives.*

An Adjective is a word which modifies the meaning of the noun, or that is used as the principal part of an uncombined attributive predicate.

Exercise.

Write five sentences in which adjectives are used to modify the meaning of the noun; five in which they are used as predicate adjectives.

We have learned that words may modify the meaning of other words by *limiting their appplication* or by *making more prominent some attribute*.

Adjectives which modify the meaning of the noun by limiting its application are called *Limiting* or *Definitive* Adjectives.

Those which modify by giving prominence to some attribute are called *Epithets*.

NOTE—The word *the* which is generally used as a limiting adjective is sometimes added to the noun without modifying its meaning in any way; as, *The* sun shines *The* earth is round. When used in this way this word is called by grammarians *a word of euphony*.

Define a predicate adjective.

Classify the adjectives in the following sentences:

The dead leaves fall. The house was cheerless. The vivid lightning flashes. Every drop is musical. That fragile violet was crushed. He is an honest man. The snow is every where. Pure water is tasteless. She found rest in the silent grave. The flowing stream is clear. Before the journey was completed, black night was upon us. Kind, loving nature covers the dead giant. The fragrant arbutus grows in New England. The trembling leaves indicate a gentle breeze. The golden ripple on the wall came back again. It is the sun, the beautiful, bright, round sun. I had a dream, a strange, wild dream. Life flowed on like a sunny, babbling brook. The solemn death watch clicked the hour she died.

"The pretty stream, the flattered stream,
The shy, yet unreluctant stream."

" An unrembered Past
Broods like a presence mid the long gray boughs
Of this old tree, which has out-lived so long
The flitting generations of mankind."

" Pale she was as the bramble blooms,
That fill the long fields with their faint perfumes."

Verbs.

We have seen that the copula of the sentence may be combined with the predicate, or it may be a separate word. Whether separate or combined the word used as the copula is called *a verb.*

A Verb is a word that is used as the copula of the sentence.

Since the copula of the sentence always expresses the relation discerned between the subject and predicate of thought the verb may be defined thus:—

A Verb is a word which expresses the relation discerned between the subject and predicate of thought.

A verb that is used only as the copula is a *Pure Verb.*

A verb that contains both copula and predicate is a *Predicate Verb* or an *Attributive Verb.*

Write five sentences containing pure verbs; five containing attributive verbs. Select ten sentences of each class from your reading lesson.

Both pure and attributive verbs may consist of more than one word; as, *will be, will be studying, is studying, shall have been, shall have been studying.* Of these examples the first and fourth are pure verbs; the second, third, and fifth are attributive verbs.

Exercise.

Point out the verbs consisting of more than one word in the following:

Classify all the verbs as Pure or Attributive.

The leaves fall. The melon is ripe. The day advances. Mary is thinking. The rain is falling. Youth fades. Summer will have passed. The grass will be green again. Many words darken speech. The sick child is patient. The trees in winter are bare. The people have been conquered. Disasters will reach both great and small. A sentence is a group of words expressing a thought. He will be returning to his home. Shining stars are worlds far off. The leaves are trembling in the wind. I have read of the luxuriant foliage of Brazil.

Adverbs and Modals.

It has been shown in the preceding exercises that attributes of concretes and abstracts are expressed by two classes of words; viz., Adjectives and Attributive Verbs.

We have also seen that there is a class of words which express attributes of other attributes. Examples.—Mary studies *faithfully.* She is *very* weak. An *unusually* large crop was produced.

The words *faithfully, very,* and *unusually*—which express attributes of other attributes—modify the meaning of the attribute words to which they are added. These words are called *Adverbs.*

An adverb is a word used to modify the meaning of an attribute word ;

or,

An adverb is a word that expresses an attribute of an attribute.

Since Adjectives, Attributive Verbs, and Adverbs express attributes, they are modified by Adverbs.

Exercise.

Point out the adverbs in the following, and state whether they modify the meaning of Adjectives, Attributive Verbs, or Adverbs:

She listens attentively. The river is very deep. A peculiarly interesting story was told. He speaks quite fluently. He was extremely prodigal. It can be defended too warmly. Those lofty trees wave proudly. The bricks are laid very firmly. Wonderfully beautiful clouds floated about the clear mountain peak. I shall study here. Human prudence should be rightly understood. A swiftly flowing stream is beautiful. She decided too hastily. They partially comprehended the question. The vine still clings to the moldering wall. Virtue is often neglected. On the north the hills rise abruptly. The hall was brilliantly illuminated and closely packed.

NOTE.—Words usually adverbs sometimes perform the office of an Adjective. When so used they should be classed as Adjectives.

EXAMPLES:—John is *here.* Henry is *there.* The words *here* and *there* are used in these sentences as predicate adjectives.

State the resemblances and differences between Adjectives and Adverbs.

From the preceding discussions it follows that all words which modify the meaning of the subject or the non-attributive predicate are Adjectives; and that those modifying Attributive predicates are Adverbs. We have yet to classify *copula modifiers*. Words used as modifiers of this element of the sentence are called *Modals*. In the sentences, "That is *probably* true" "*Perhaps* he will go." "The report is *probably* incorrect," the words *possibly, perhaps,* and *probably* are used as *Modals*.

A **Modal** is a word used to modify the meaning of the copula.

Exercise.

Distinguish the Modals from the Adverbs in the following sentences:

It is certainly late. The rose is delicately tinted. He spoke truly. Truly, God is good. Undoubtedly, it is a difficult task. Perhaps I shall go to-morrow. The sun will surely rise. He finally started. Possibly, we may fail. Henry is nearly over the Atlantic. They will assuredly be destroyed. I am not going. He is truly brave. The story really is true. The story is really true.

Phrases and clauses may be used as *Adjectives, Adverbs,* or *Modals*.

Examples.—We left *on Tuesday*. We shall go *when you come*. The story *without doubt* is false. I shall go *if you remain*. *Had he inquired* he would have learned. A man *of straw* was prostrated. Ships *that ply about Cape Horn* must be strongly built.

Preposition.

"The house is *on the hill*." "The book *on the table* is mine."

The predicate phrase *on the hill* expresses an attribute of relation of the object house. The word *on* which is a part of this phrase shows relation between the objects *house* and *hill*. The phrase *on the table* is a modifying phrase, and the word *on* shows the relation between the objects *book* and *table*. In the sentence, "John spoke to James," the word *to* forms part of a modifying phrase and shows the relation between the attribute expressed in the word *spoke* and the object *James*. "John is better than Henry." Here the word *better* forms part of a phrase and shows relation between two objects.

The words *on*, *to*, and *better* are alike in that each forms a part of a phrase, and is a relation word. The word *better* is unlike the other two words in that it expresses an attribute. The words *on* and *to* show relation without expressing an attribute. Such words as *on* and *to* are called *Prepositions*.

A Preposition is a relation word that forms part of a phrase and does not express an attribute.

Exercise.

Point out the prepositions in the following, and state whether they form parts of principal or modifying phrases. Designate the objects or the object and the attribute between which the prepositions show relation:

The pencil is black. The sun is in the heavens. Burton went to Philadelphia. The leaves of the trees are withered and dry. The dog swam across the river. My sister is at home. I study at school. They traveled over mountains. I bring fresh flowers from the sea. The forces of Hannibal were routed by Scipio. The sun is shining through the shower. The meadow is enameled with clover blossoms. The steed along the drawbridge flies. The bees find honey in the fragrant flowers. He spoke to John about his brother. That woman was the mother of George Washington. The woods against the stormy sky, their giant branches tossed.

> " From the hill-top looked the steeple
> And the light-house from the strand,
> And the scattered pines are waving
> Their farewell from the land."

> "Our lives are rivers, gliding free,
> To that unfathomed, boundless sea."

A phrase containing a preposition is called a *prepositional phrase* or an *adjunct*.

Write five sentences in which prepositional phrases shall be used as the principal part of the predicate; five in which they shall be used as modifying parts of the predicate; and five in which they shall be used as modifying parts of the subject.

Conjunction.

State how many thoughts are expressed in each of the following sentences and tell what words show that these thoughts are connected:

The day dawned and we started. We must educate or we must perish. I go, but I return. He is happy because he is good. She works though she is ill. John will go, but Mary will stay. He was poor though he might have been rich.

The sentence, "John and James are studious," expresses two thoughts. That which is alike in both—the predicate—is expressed but once. If the two thoughts were expressed in full, the sentence would read—"John is studious and James is studious." The word *and* is used to show that the thoughts are connected.

The sentence, "John and James are a handsome couple," expresses but a single thought; the predicate could not be affirmed of either John or James alone. The words *John* and *James* are both required to express the entire subject. Neither word however, modifies the meaning of the other; they are both required to form the principal part of the subject;—they express objects that are co-ordinate parts of the subject of thought. The connection of these coordinate parts is expressed by the word *and*.

In the sentence, "Air is oxygen and nitrogen," the word *and* is used to show connection between co-ordinate parts of the predicate of thought.

These connecting words are called *Conjunctions*.

A Conjunction is a word used to show connection between thoughts, or between coordinate parts of the same element of thought.

Exercise.

Point out the conjunctions in the following, and state whether they show connection between thoughts, or between coordinate parts of the same element of thought:

Mary learns easily, but she forgets soon. Mary and Jane study together. The pinks and the roses are fragrant. That is a red and white flower. Birds chirp and sing. Five and four make nine. You and I are going. We find flowers in the woods and by the streams. The great statesman and orator is dead. The moon and stars are shining. Bread and milk is excellent food for children. You may buy books or slates. A large and beautiful horse was killed. It is a hard case, still there is help for it. Henry and James are well matched. The scholar and poet was also the christian and patriot. The prudent and diligent man prospers. John and James are diligent. John and James are united in their opinions. The government is constituted of the executive, the legislative, and the judical departments. A belt of trees and shrubs conceals the fence. Wheat and rye will germinate in a single day. Action and contemplation are in no way inconsistent. Man is head, body, and limbs. Plato and Socrates were Athenians. The wall is brick and mortar. Our trials and dangers abound.

Interjection.

There is another class of words such as *oh, alas, ah, hurrah*, and others, whose use is to express feeling. The feelings expressed by these words are not elements of the thought, hence the words themselves form no part of the sentence. They are called *Interjections*.

An Interjection is a word used to express feeling and which does not form a part of the sentence.

Give the literal meaning of the words *noun, pronoun, adjective, verb, adverb, modal, preposition, conjunction,* and *interjection*.

The different classes of words we have studied are shown in the following diagram:

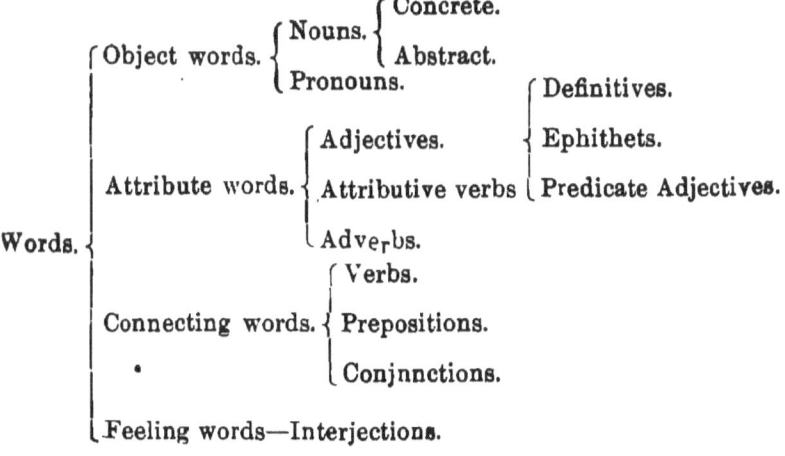

NOTE.—Frequent exercises in the analysis of sentences should be given, which should be sufficiently exhaustive to test the pupils knowledge of the different classes of words used in the sentence. To avoid making the exercises too long the analysis might be limited to one or two elements, or to one or two classes of words.

"The large man spoke harshly to the little child."

The words *The large man* form the logical subject of this sentence. The word *spoke* is both the logical and the grammatical copula. The logical predicate consists of the words *spoke harshly to the little child*. The word *spoke*, is the grammatical predicate. The grammatical subject—the word *man*—names a concrete object, hence is a concrete noun. The modifying parts of the subject—the words *the* and *large*—are used to limit the application of the noun man, hence are definitive adjectives. The adjective *large* limits by expressing an attribute that does not belong to the whole class of men and the word *the* by pointing out a particular one of the class of large men. The grammatical predicate, "spoke," is attributive and is combined with the copula, hence it is an attributive verb.. The modifying part of the predicate consists of an attributive modifier—the word *harshly*—and an indirect objective modifier—the words *the little child*. The word *harshly* modifies the meaning of the word spoke by expressing an attribute of the attribute, hence is an adverb. The principal part of the objective modifier—the word *child* is a concrete noun. The words *the* and *little* modify the meaning of the noun child by limiting its application, hence they are definitive adjectives. The word *to* is used to show relation between the attribute *spoke* and the object *child*, hence is a preposition.

"They departed silently, at night." The predicate of this sentence, the word *departed*, is attributive and is combined with the copula. It contains two attributive modifiers,—the word *silently* which expresses an attribute of quality of the action *departed*, and the phrase *at night* which expresses an attribute of relation to time.

"The stream slides over the ledges and dips in the basin." This sentence contains two verbs, two prepositions and one conjunction. The verbs *dips* and *slides* are both attributive. The preposition *over* shows the relation between the attribute *slides* and the object *ledges*. The word *in* shows relation between this same attribute and the object *basin*. The conjunction *and* shows connection between the thoughts—*The stream slides over ledges*, and *The stream drips in the basin*.

NOTE.—When the sub-classes of words, and their grammatical attributes are earned, more can be told of both principal and modifying parts.

CHAPTER VII.

CLASSES OF NOUNS.

Concrete objects having one or more like attributes are on account of their likeness brought together in thought and viewed as forming a whole called a *class*. John, James and Henry are all *devoted to study*; because of their likeness in this respect they are classed together; the name of this class is *student*. These same persons may be *eminent for political abilities*; because they all have this attribute they are put in the class *statesman*. Persons having in common the attribute of being *engaged in military service* form the class *soldier*. Objects having the power of voluntary motion form the class *animal*.

A noun naming a class is called a *class noun*. The nouns *student, statesman, soldier* and *animal* are class nouns.

Each individual of the class having all the attributes that give rise to the class, bears the class name. John, James and Henry may each bear the names *student* and *statesman*.

A Class Noun is a noun that names a class and belongs equally to all the individuals composing the class.

NOTE.—The class noun is sometimes called a *common noun* because it belongs in common to all the individuals of the class.

Exercise.

Write five sentences in which the class noun is used as the principal part of the subject; five in which it is used as the principal part of the predicate. Point out the nouns thus used and state of each whether it is applied to the whole class, or to one or more of the individuals composing the class.

Examples.—"The dog, the horse and the elephant are teachable and intelligent." "The boys are playing." "That is a new house." In the first sentence, the class nouns *dog, horse* and *elephant*, are each used to apply to the whole class; the noun *boys* applies to two or more individuals of the class, and the noun *house* to one of the class.

Besides having a name in common with the other members of the class each individual has a *special* name, given to it to distinguish it from the other individuals of the class. The names *New York*,

Boston, and *Chicago,* are special names given to different individuals belonging to the class *city.* Such names are called *Proper Nouns.*

A Proper Noun is a special name given to an individual of a class to distinguish it from other individuals of the same class.

Exercise.

Point out the proper nouns in the following, and state to what class each object named belongs:

Italy contains many celebrated cities. The Alps are in Switzerland. The Danube is in Europe. Cora is attentive. Venus revolves about the sun. The St. Clair was burned on Lake Superior. Carlo barks. Dobbin prances. December is cold.

Example.—" Sunday was very warm." The word Sunday is a proper noun; it names a certain day of the week.

NOTE—A proper noun becomes a class noun when it is viewed as the common name of two or more individuals.

Example. He was the *Cicero* of the age. The *Johns* are industrious.

Concrete objects collected together in space form a whole called a *group* or *collection.* The noun naming such a whole is a *Collective noun.* The noun *swarm* names a group of insects; the noun *grove* a small collection of trees; the noun *forest* names a large collection of trees. These nouns are *collective* nouns.

A Collective Noun is the name of a group or collection of objects.

NOTE 1.—We have seen that the class noun will apply to any individual of the class. The collective noun will not apply to one of the group; we cannot say of one insect of the swarm that it is *a swarm,* nor of one tree of a grove that it is *a grove.* The objects forming a group are collected together in space; those forming a class may or may not exist together; the basis of their union is the attributes which they have in common; they may exist apart, yet if they are found to be alike in one or more respects they are thought as belonging to the same class.

NOTE 2.—A collective noun may become a class noun. When so viewed the individuals composing the class are groups.

EXAMPLE.—"Several *parties* of visitors arrived." In the phrase, "A large flock of birds," the word *flock* is a class noun if the mind is considering the flock named as distinguished from other flocks; if the idea of the group is more prominent it is a collective noun.

State the resemblances and differences between a class and a collective noun.

A concrete object may be viewed simply as a being—a material—a substance—or a mass.

Examples.—*Gold* is valuable. *Iron* is heavy. *Wheat* is abundant. The nouns *gold*, *iron* and *wheat* name objects viewed in this way.

Such nouns are called *Mass* or *Material* nouns.

A Mass Noun is the name of an object viewed simply as a being or material.

NOTE 1.—The nouns *mind* and *spirit* are *mass* nouns. The objects named by these nouns do not occupy space, but we think of them in the same way that we think of objects having extension.

NOTE 2.—Mass nouns may be used as class nouns.

Examples.—Mountain *air*. Ripe *wheat*. Fresh *water*.

Exercise.

Classify the nouns in the following :

Patagonia is an unsettled region. A milkmaid poised a full pail on her head. The crowd was large. Snow is white. A hundred birds are singing as birds never sing except in the morning. God is eternal. Napoleon died at St. Helena. The northern States produce wheat, oats, rye, barley and, corn. A host so great as covered all the field. A great multitude was assembled. Down comes the flood, and every drop is musical. A pair of birds built their nest in the tallest tree. Christmas comes but once a year. Air, earth, and water teem with delight. Here they raised their little family. A Persian resolved to divide his goods among his sons. A couple of dogs barked furiously. The school was dismissed. I trudged off through the woods and meadows. Gold and silver are valuable. Water is a fluid. The army landed at the foot of the cliff. Spirit is active; matter inert.

Abstract nouns are of four classes, viz.; Quality Nouns, Condition Nouns, Action Nouns and Relation Nouns.

Upon what is the classification of Abstract nouns based ?

Exercise.

Classify the abstract nouns in the following:

Brightness belongs to the sun. Sleep is refreshing. Running is tiresome. The nearness of the countries makes intercourse easy. His intelligence is remarkable. After a short struggle they yielded. Great was the grief among the village school boys. His influence is not questioned. The beauty of the landscape was pleasing. After deliberation she resolved to save her brother. The necessity for cleanliness is apparent. They have particular confidence in man. For the strength of the hills we bless thee. Let us share in the rapture of heaven and earth. Men have done brave deeds. We feel our own inferiority. The steamy air is all with fragrance rife. Proclaim liberty throughout all the land. The motion of the boat lulled him to rest. To the spirit belongs control. When the first soft days of spring come in all their gentle sweetness, and woo us with their warmth, and soothe us with their smile, then come the birds. Bitter mourning on the night wind rose and fell. Sickness and sorrow left their traces on her face. Is it to force us back to submission? Wild joy possessed each mariner's breast. Its magical call awakens the flowerets. Ask yourselves how this gracious reception of our petition comports with these warlike preparations.

Change all the abstract nouns in the preceding exercise to forms that express attributes proper.

Abstract nouns may be used as Class or as Proper nouns.

Examples.—His *actions* were inconsistent. Vegetable *growth* is effected by absorption and circulation. *Faith*, *Hope*, and *Charity* are virtues. *Truth*, *Beauty*, and *Goodness* are excellencies.

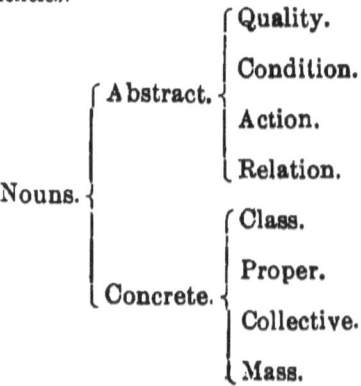

CHAPTER VIII.

CLASSES OF ADJECTIVES.

We have seen that all adjectives are modifying or predicate adjectives; and that modifying adjectives are either *definitives* or *epithets*.

Both definitives and epithets may be divided into smaller classes.

A definitive may limit the application of the noun by expressing *quantity;* as, *much* snow; *six* men; *many* books. These adjectives express quantity in the *mass* or *bulk*, as in the first example, or quantity in number—numerical quantity—as in the last two examples.

Exercise.

Point out the adjectives in the following phrases, and state whether they express quantity in the mass, or numerical quantity; and whether the numerical quantity is expressed definitely or indefinitely:

Eight days. Few persons. Many houses. Either book. Neither book. Four lilies. Some water. Some pencils. Any city. Any snow. All men. Enough rain. Enough houses. Every child. Both hands. Several trees. No wood. No desks. Much gold. Little silver. All things. Six hundred years. Whole amount. Whole number.

Adjectives that express quantitity are called *quantitative adjectives* or *adjectives of quantity*.

Those expressing quantity in the mass are called *mass adjectives*. Those expressing numerical quantity are called *numeral adjectives*. Numeral adjectives are *definite* or *indefinite* according as they express a definite or an indefinite number.

Write five sentences containing mass adjectives; five containing definite numerals; five containing indefinite numerals.

Mass adjectives limit what kind of nouns? Numeral adjectives limit what kind of nouns?

Define an adjective of quantity; a mass adjective; a numeral adjective.

NOTE.—The *distributives, each, every, either, neither,* etc., are numerals; some of them are definite, others are indefinite. The other classes of definite numerals are the *cardinals, one, two, three,* etc., and the *multiplicatives, single, double, twofold, threefold,* etc.

NOTE 2.—The definite numerals *a* and *an* are two forms of the same word. *A* is used before words commencing with a consonant sound; as *a* book, *a* hero, *a* scholar. *An* is used before a vowel sound and before an aspirated *h* in an unaccented syllable; as *an* ocean, *an* hour, *an* heroic act.

Exercise.

Correct the errors that occur in the following phrases:

An hundred men. Such an one. A old man. A inch. A book. A honorable man. An elegant carriage. An heroine. A adjective. A historian. A honor. An humble heart. A happy life. A herbarium. An useful exercise. An union. An holy man. An hireling. An empire. An hypothetical cause. A harmonious family. An official statement.

A definitive may limit the application of the noun by pointing out the particular individual or individuals meant; as, *this* book; *those* trees; *yonder* house. Adjective that limit in this way are called *demonstratives.*

A Demonstrative is an adjective that limits the application of the noun by pointing out.

NOTE.—To this class belong the *ordinals, first, second, third,* etc. The adjective *the* when used as a definitive is also a demonstrative. It sometimes points out an individual; as, The horse is running: and sometimes a class; as, The horse is a quadruped. The word *the* is a less emphatic form of *that.*

Write five sentences containing demonstratives, and designate.

Some definitives limit the application of the noun to a certain kind or class of objects, by expressing an attribute that does not belong to the entire class named by the noun; as, *diligent* pupils; *tall* men; *dark* days. Such adjectives may be called *class* adjectives.

A *Class adjective* is one that limits the application of the noun to a certain kind of objects.

Write five sentences containing class adjectives.

NOTE.—Nouns are sometimes used as class adjectives; as, a *gold* ring; *sea* water; *house* plants.

Nouns and pronouns denoting possession are used adjectively. In this use they are still called nouns and pronouns because they express concrete and abstract objects.

An adjective may be used as a noun; as, the *righteous*; the *rich*; the *poor*.

Exercise.

Classify the adjectives in the following:

A dozen apples. These pictures. Much air. Warm weather. Gloomy thoughts. A former message. Yonder house. The same man. Sweet apples. Little money. Horse cars. Imagine a thousand pictures of birds. That *new* volume is the latest edition. The entrance has a large double door. Many beautiful dwellings were destroyed. The old elm tree has fallen. The frost looked forth one still, clear night. The myriad lights bewildered him. It sought its final resting place. All the feathery throng shall taste the spirit of spring. The last stars were vanishing. The wigwam blaze beamed on the tender and helpless. They looked like little, floating, fairy isles of sapphire. The yellow foam was splashed to the tops of the highest turrets. All Rome sent forth a rapturous cry. Fairy faces shine in heaven's most distant places.

"Fill every golden hour!
The glorious privilege to do,
Is man's most noble dower."

Adjectives.
- Modifying.
  - Definitives.
    - Quantitative.
      - Mass.
      - Numerals.
        - Definite.
        - Indefinite.
    - Demonstratives.
    - Class.
  - Epithets.
- Predicate.

CLASSES OF ADVERBS.

We have seen that the adverbs are attribute words, which modify the meaning of other attribute words.

An Adverb may modify the meaning of another attribute word expressing a quality of the attribute, as: He acted *wisely*. Mary sings well. The children move gently. An adverb used in this way is called an adverb of Quality or Manner.

Adverbs may also be used to express *amount, extent, degree,* or *intensity;* as, *much, more, less, wholly, enough, widely, equally, very, exceedingly, greatly, vehemently.*

They may express relation to place; as *here, there, hither, next;* or they may express relation to time; as, *now, then, hereafter, repeatedly, always, seldom, first, secondly, once.*

Exercise.

Write two sentences containing adverbs of manner; two containing adverbs of amount; two containing adverbs expressing relation to place; two containing adverbs expressing relation to time. Designate.

NOTE.—Phrases and clauses may be used to modify attribute words; as "The child died *of hunger.*" "I shall go *when the boat arrives.*" A single word performing the office of an *adverb*, is called simply an *adverb*. Phrases and clauses performing the same office are called *adverbials*.

The phrase *of hunger*, and the clause *when the boat arrives*, are adverbials.

The adverbial *of hunger* expresses an attribute of relation of *cause and effect*. The adverbial *when the boat arrives* is an adverbial of relation to time.

Exercise.

Classify the adverbs and adverbials in the following:

She spoke gently. I shall go instantly. The task is nearly done. He finally went. They came twice. You should write legibly and spell correctly. They were wholly overcome. The orator spoke vehemently. He was widely known. You are much deceived. The books are equally good. I will study more diligently. That man is much respected. They came twice. He was greatly blessed. You have studied enough. He will work to-morrow. I never saw a more industrious person. The stage started early. Duty is often neglected. The water flows there. Rudely blows the winter blast. The task was exceedingly difficult. I have been too idle. The weather is very cold. James spoke too abruptly. The boy is sitting there. The work is almost finished. They went silently at night. The house stood by the river. Her mother died when she was a child. Some trees are green throughout the year. She fainted from fright. You wrote in haste. I live in this place.

Write five sentences containing adverbial phrases; five containing adverbial clauses.

CHAPTER IX.

CLASSES OF PREPOSITIONS.

There are many different kinds of relations between objects and between attributes and objects that may be shown by prepositions; this gives rise to many classes of relation words. The following is a list of some of the classes of relations shown by prepositions, with the words used to indicate these relations:

RELATIONS TO PLACE: (a) *Position;* as, *at, on, by, beyond, before, after, among, against, beneath, besides, behind.* (b.) *Direction;* as, *down, up, toward, to, along, across, through.*

RELATIONS TO TIME: as, *at, after, before, during, till, between.*

SOURCE, QUALITY, POSSESSION, or CAUSE: as, *from, of, because.*

MOTIVE or AIM: as, Miners delve *for* gold.

RESULT: as, The man was frightened *to* death.

MEANS or INSTRUMENT: Done *by* strategy. Written *with* a pen.

ACCOMPANIMENT or CONNECTION: as, John went *with* his brother.

EXCLUSION: as, All went *but* James.

IDENTITY: as, The island *of* Sicily.

Exercise.

Classify the prepositions in exercise on page 21.

NOTE.—The same preposition may be used to show different kinds of relation; as, "The children are *at* school.'" "They came *at* six o'clock." In the first sentence the word *at* is used to indicate a relation to place; in the second sentence the same word is used to show a relation to time.

NOTE 2.—The two objects, or the attribute and the object, between which the preposition shows a relation are called the *terms* of the relation. The object or attribute *of* which the preposition shows a relation is called the *antecedent* term of the relation, and the object *to* which the preposition shows a relation is called the *subsequent* term of the relation.

Exercise.

(a.) Point out the words in the following expressing the antecedent term of the relation indicated by the preposition, and those expressing the subsequent term:

(b.) Classify the prepositions, and state whether they form parts of principal or of modifying phrases:

We went in the morning. The cattle are in the field. A tempest swept over the forest. There is much discouragement among the soldiers. I write with a pen. The rays of the sun are piercing. Seek for a higher life. The man is dying of fever. Everything was done in silence. The attack was made with great vehemence. She is writing at the house of her brother. The farmer cuts grass with a scythe. I went with my mother. The cars go from New York towards Boston. The question of order was next discussed. The wealth of the people was great. The youngest son of the king claimed the throne. A man of generosity would have done differently. Work for some worthy end. The man was imprisoned for debt. The flash of their muskets lighted the street. The stars of heaven shall guide us. The island of Corsica is in the Mediterranean.

CHAPTER X.

CLASSES OF CONJUNCTIONS.

We have seen that conjunctions are words which show relation between thoughts. There are different classes of these relations, hence there are different classes of conjunctions. Some conjunctions simply indicate that two thoughts are connected; as, The pencil *and* the book are on the table; others show the kind of relation existing between the thoughts connected. Those of the first class are called COPULATIVES. Contained under the second class are,—

1. ILLATIVES;—those which show that one judgment is the reason for, or the consequence of the other; as, I study *because* I must. It rains, *therefore* the ground is wet.

2. DISJUNCTIVES;—those which show that the relation between two judgments is that of alternation; as, We must study *or* we must fail. I have not tears *nor* pity for him.

3. ADVERSATIVES;—those which indicate that two judgments are

opposed, or that one judgment is opposed to a conclusion that may be drawn from the other; as, I go *but* I return. *Though* he studies, he does not learn.

4. CONDITIONALS;—those which indicate that one judgment is the ground or condition for the other; as, *If* it rain, I shall not go. Here the judgment expressed in the first sentence is the ground or condition for the judgment expressed in the second sentence.

5. CLAUSAL CONJUCTIONS;—those which indicate that one judgment is viewed as an object and is an element of another judgment; as, *That* the earth is round is believed. We all know *that* war is a calamity. Here the judgment expressed in the clause, *the earth is round*, is the subject of thought; that expressed by the clause, *war is a calamity*, is the object of the attribute *know*.

NOTE 1.—*Copulatives, disjunctives, adversatives* and *illatives* all show relation between thoughts that are co-ordinate, hence they are called co-ordinate conjunctions. *Conditional* and *clausal* conjunctions differ from these in that they show relation between thoughts that are not co-ordinate: the clause introduced by a conditional conjunction is a copula modifier—a modal; that introduced by a clausal conjunction is a noun. Neither of the sentences expressing thoughts whose relation is shown by a co-ordinate conjuction forms a part of the other.

NOTE 2.—The words *and, also, furthermore, besides, likewise,* and others are used as Copulative Conjunctions; *because, for, as, therefore, since,* and *consequently,* are used as Illatives; *or* and *nor* are used as Disjunctives; *but, still, yet, though, nevertheless,* and *although* are Adversatives; *if* and *provided* are Conditionals; *that, whether* and *if* are used as Clausal Conjunctions.

Exercises.

(a) Use the conjunctions just named, in written sentences.

(b) Write two sentences in which a clause introduced by a clausal conjunction is used as the subject of a sentence; two in which such a clause is used as the predicate; two in which it is used as an objective modifier.

(c) Classify the conjunctions in the following:

The sun and the moon stood still. James or his sister will come. You should not waste your words nor your time. As the wind is favorable the ship will sail soon. We went notwithstanding it rained. You will be despised and he will be honored. Success is difficult because many strive. I know not if it be so. Snow or rain may be expected. Rise, for it is day. Touch it not, lest ye die. Rome must destroy Carthage or Carthage will be a perpetual threat to Rome. The man is sick, consequently he needs help. His father pleaded with him but he would not listen. Either the universe had a creator, or it exists by chance. They found ruin yet they were not cast down. That the earth revolves no one doubts. Since you insist upon it I consent. He said that he would go. All day long they were busy yet they never failed to warble. His step was firm and his figure erect, though he seemed old and wayworn. I have believed, therefore I have spoken. I know that I have not much to recommend me, nevertheless I wish to be loved. If all be well we shall leave home next week. Whether he has arrived is not known. The wind has changed but it continues to rain. He said nothing more, nor did I. If it had been necessary he would have sacrificed his life.

CHAPTER XI.

CLASSES OF SENTENCES.

Simple, Compound and Complex.

State which of the following sentences express but one thought and which express two or more co-ordinate thoughts:

War has ceased. War has ceased and peace has come. Spring comes and the flowers bloom. A soft answer turneth away wrath, but grievous words stir up anger. None will flatter the poor. Talent is power, but tact is skill. James and Mary go to school. Cats and dogs are domestic animals. The sun warms and lights. You must pay gold or silver. The seasons came, went, and came again.

A sentence expressing but a single thought is a *simple* sentence; one expressing two or more co-ordinate thoughts is a *Compound* sentence.

A Simple Sentence is one that expresses but a single thought.

A Compound Sentence is one that expresses two or more co-ordinate thoughts.

We have seen that the simple sentence may have its elements made up of co-ordinate parts; (*See p. 22.*) Any element of a sentence—principal or modifying—that contains co-ordinate parts, is a compound element. In the sentence, "You and I will read together," the principal part of the subject is compound; it consists of the co-ordinate parts "You" and "I;" the predicate can not be affirmed of either part alone. "The book is cover and leaves;" here the principal part of the predicate is compound; we can not say "The book is cover," or "The book is leaves." "A black and white shawl was worn:" here the modifying part of the subject is compound; while in the sentence, "She wore a black and white shawl," the modifying part of the predicate is compound.

Exercises.

(a). State which of the sentences in exercise, page 22, are compound, and which are simple sentences with compound elements.

(b). State which element of the simple sentences is compound.

(c). Write five compound sentences; two simple sentences with compound subjects; two with compound predicates; two with compound modifiers.

"It is, I think, the best that can be done."
"This is, in a word, the true condition of affairs."
"My lads, I have done."
"John, study."
"He is, John says, very industrious."

By observing these sentences it may be seen that they differ from those we have studied, in that each has joined to it a part which is not its co-ordinate, and which forms no part of either the subject, the predicate, or the copula. The first sentence has joined to it the words "I think." Combined with the second sentence is the phrase, "in a word." The forms of address, "My lads," and "John," do not belong to any element of the sentences to which they are joined. "John says," is not co-ordinate with the sentence to which it is joined, and does not form a part of the subject, the predicate, or the copula.

A sentence having joined to it a part which is not co-ordinate, and which forms no part of either the subject, the predicate, or the copula, is a COMPLEX SENTENCE.

NOTE.—A sentence in which a clause is used as an element is commonly called a complex sentence; but a clause thus used performs the office of a single word, and is regarded simply as a part of speech; the sentence is not made complex by its introduction. Examples—"He *who is industrious* will succeed." "Flowers bloom *when spring returns.*" "I believe *he is honest.*" These sentences are all simple; the clause "who is industrious," is used as an adjective; "when spring returns," is used as an adverb; "he is honest" is used as an objective modifier.

Exercise.

Distinguish the sentences in the following as simple, compound, or complex.

Avarice causes crime. The patient ox submits to the yoke, and meekly performs his labor. He who conquers his passions, overcomes his greatest enemies. I love thee, winter. Prosperity gains many friends, but adversity tries them. I know they will come. This is, said James, all I have. I disregard their imputations, because I do not merit them. To be candid, I can not believe it. When he had sold his patrimony, he engaged in traffic. Mother, he faintly said, come near me. He might have been guilty, but no sufficient proof could be found. The time, I say, has come. Nature never did betray the heart that loved her. I know that my redeemer liveth.

"Soft is the strain when zephyr gently blows,
And the smooth stream in smoother numbers flows."

Declarative, Interrogative, Imperative and Exclamatory.

The sentence, "The apple is sweet," shows that the mind discerns that sweetness belongs to the object apple; i. e., it shows that the relation between the subject and the predicate of thought is known —determined. The sentence, "Glass is not opaque," also expresses this relation as determined; but the sentence, "Is the apple sweet?" shows that the relation between the subject and predicate of thought is undetermined, and that the mind seeks to know this relation.

When the relation between the subject and the predicate of thought is expressed as known, the judgment is called a determined judgment; when it is unknown and sought for, the judgment is called an undetermined judgment.

Express in written sentences five determined and five undetermined judgments.

Any element of the thought may be undetermined. The sentence, "Who struck John?" shows that the subject is unknown and sought for; the sentence, "Where is the book?" indicates that the predicate is undetermined; while the sentence, "What did he break?" shows that a part of the predicate—the object—is undetermined.

A determined judgment is expressed is what is called a *Declarative sentence*; an undetermined judgment, or a judgment is which some element is undetermined and sought for is expressed in an *Interrogative* sentence —a question.

A Declarative Sentence is one that expresses a determined judgment.

Or,

A Declarative Sentence is one that shows that the relation between the thought subject and the thought predicate is determined.

An Interrogative Sentence is one that expresses an undetermined judgment, or a judgment in which some element is undetermined and sought for.

Or,

An Interrogative Sentence is one that shows that some element of the thought is undetermined and sought for.

Exercise.

Write five declarative sentences. Write two interrogative sentences showing that the subject of thought is undetermined; two showing that the predicate is undetermined; and two showing that the relation between the subject and the predicate is undetermined.

A sentence may express peremptory will; i. e., a command; as, "Be quiet." "Attend to your own work." "Go." Such sentences are called *Imperative sentences.*

An Imperative Sentence is one which expresses a command.

Besides expressing thought the sentence sometimes expresses *feeling.* If the feeling expressed is more prominent than the thought the sentence is called an *Exclamatory* or *Emotive sentence*; as, "How glad I am to see you!"

An Exclamatory or Emotive Sentence is one in which the feeling expressed is more prominent than the thought.

Exercise.

Classify the following sentences, and state, of each interrogative sentence, what element of the thought expressed in it is represented as undetermined·

I am a poor man. Is the room warm? Who will go for us? How frightful the grave! Which is John? Bring me that book. Whose book have you brought? Clarence is come! Attend to your work. What will you take? How beautiful upon the mountains are the feet of him that bringeth good tidings! When shall it be morn in the grave? I shall go to-morrow. What will you take? Speak softly. Shall I return the book? Calm was the day. Am I requested to go? Children, obey your parents. Oh, that those lips had language! Do you believe that the voyage will restore your health? And Ardennes waves above them her green leaves. Go in peace. Whose book is this? Look round thee. Charge, Chester, charge! Was it from Heaven?

> "Tell me not in mournful numbers
> Life is but an empty dream."

NOTE.—All sentences should be commenced with a capital letter. Declarative and Imperative sentences should be finished with a period. Interrogative sentences should be finished with an interrogation point, and Exclamatory sentences with an exclamation point. When the name of the object addressed is used in connection with an imperative sentence, it should be separated from the sentence by a comma. If the element which renders the sentence complex is placed between parts of the sentence, a comma should be placed both before and after it.

Exercise.

Capitalize and punctuate the following sentences correctly:

has the king a right to transfer the crown the great golden eagle stooped down and flew away with something in his talons how beautiful is all this visible world cast your eyes sir over this extensive country cowley indeed used to call himself melancholy what terrors round him wait is this the character of british justice my lord we have stood here observing him how uncertain is human life

CHAPTER XI.

ANALYSIS.

Analysis is the separation of a sentence into its elements.

Before a sentence is analyzed it should be determined:

(a.) Whether it is simple, compound or complex;

(b.) Whether it is declarative, interrogative, imperative, or exclamatory.

The following method is suggested for the classification and analysis of sentences:

(a.) State whether the sentence is simple, compound, or complex.

(b.) State whether it is declarative, interrogative, imperative, or exclamatory.

(c.) Name the three logical elements.

(d.) Name the principal and modifying parts of each of these elements.

(e.) Name the principal and modifying parts of each modifying element:—(1) of the subject; (2) of the predicate; (3) of the copula. Classify each word.

(f.) If the principal or modifying part of any element is a clause or a phrase, after referring it as a whole to the part of speech to which it belongs, separate it into its elements.

(g.) If the sentence is compound, analyze each simple sentence of which it is composed, and classify the connecting words.

(h.) If the sentence is complex, name the sentence proper and the element which makes it complex, and analyze each.

(i.) Classify all the parts of speech.

Example.

"The sumptuous cities which have lighted the world since the beginning of time, are now beheld only in the pictures of the historian or the poet."

This is a simple declarative sentence. "The sumptuous cities which have lighted the world since the beginning of time" is the logical subject; "are now beheld only in the pictures of the historian or the poet" is the logical predicate; the grammatical and logical copula are combined with the grammatical predicate in the words "are beheld."

The noun "cities" is the grammatical subject modified by the adjective "sumptuous;" "sumptuous cities" is modified by the adjective "the;" "the sumptuous cities" is modified by the adjective clause "which have lighted the world since the beginning of time;" the pronoun "which" is the grammatical and logical subject of this clause; "have lighted the world since the beginning of time" is the logical predicate; the verb "have lighted" is the copula and the grammatical predicate combined. As predicate, "have lighted" is modified by the objective phrase "the world;" the noun "world" is modified by the adjective "the;" "have lighted the world" is also modified by the adverbial phrase "since the beginning of time;" the principal part of this phrase is the noun "beginning," which is modified by the adjective "the;" "the beginning" is modified by the adjective phrase "of time;" the principal part of this phrase is the noun "time;" "of" is a preposition expressing the relation of "beginning" to "time;" "since" is a preposition expressing the relation of "have lighted the world" to "the beginning of time." "Are beheld" as grammatical predicate is modified by the adverb "now;" "are now beheld" is modified by the adjective phrase, "in the pictures of the historian or the poet;" the noun "pictures," the principal part of the phrase, is modified by the adjective "the;" "the pictures" is modified by the compound adjective element "of the historian or the poet;" the nouns "historian" and "poet" are each modified by the adjective "the;" "of" is a preposition showing the relation of "pictures" to "historian;" "in" is a preposition showing the relation of "are now beheld" to "the pictures of the historian or poet;" "only" is an adverb modifying the adverbial phrase" in the pictures of the historian or the poet."

A more common method of analyzing the above sentence is as follows:

After classifying the sentence and stating the logical subject, predicate, and copula, proceed as follows:

The grammatical subject is the noun "cities," modified by the adjectives "the" and "sumptuous," and by the adjective clause, "which have lighted the world since the beginning of time;" of this clause the pronoun "which" is the logical and grammatical subject, and "have lighted" is the grammatical predicate; "have lighted" is modified by the noun "world," which is modified by the adjective "the;" the predicate is also modified by the adverbial phrase "since the beginning of time;" the noun "beginning" is modified by the adjective "the" and the adjective phrase "of time." "Are beheld," the grammatical predicate is modified by the adverbs "now" and "only," and the adverbial phrase "in the pictures of the historian or the poet;" the principal part of this phrase, the noun "pictures," is modified by the adjective "the" and the compound adjective phrase "of the historian or the poet;" the nouns "historian" and "poet" are each modified by the adjective "the."

This latter method of analysis may be expressed by a diagram as follows :

```
           ⎧ the
           ⎪ sumptuous
     Cities⎨
           ⎪ ⎧ which
           ⎩ ⎨                ⎧ world ⎨ the         ⎨ the
             ⎩ have lighted ⎨        ⎨ (since) beginning ⎨ (of) time;

              ⎧ now
              ⎪ only           ⎧ the
  are beheld ⎨                ⎨              ⎧ historian ⎨ the
              ⎩ (in) pictures ⎩ (of)         ⎨ (or)
                                             ⎩ poet      ⎨ the.
```

The first method is preferable because the pupil is compelled to determine every step by a careful analysis of the thought. It is probable, however, that the results obtained will not be so uniform as in the less complicated method; but this is not of so much importance as that the pupils shall be taught to see the influence of word, phrase, or clause, in modifying the thought.

Exercise.

Analyze the following sentences:

In the reign of Henry II all foreign commodities were plenty in England. After I had visited Europe, I returned to America. Remember that you may be disappointed in your plans. I told him that I would go. Travelers can ascend by a winding road to the top of Mt. Washington. The climate of Florida is favorable to invalids. On Prague's proud arch the fires of ruin glow. The credulity which has faith in goodness is a sign of goodness. The noble Brutus hath told you Cæsar was ambitious. This hour's work will breed proscriptions. The brilliant flowers of the tropics bloom from the windows of the green-house. Rays which fall perpendicularly upon the earth are called vertical. "My son," said he, "did you ever hear of any who are called ungrateful?" He who openly tells his friends all that he thinks of them, must expect that they will secretly tell his enemies much that they do not think of him. They were united by ties of friendship and of kindred. One day the poor woman and her idiot boy were missed from the market-place. He gained from heaven, 'twas all he wished, a friend. The first works of the imagination are, as we have said, poor and rude. Peace rules the day, when reason rules the mind. Scarce would they see or hear their foes. Down bend the banks; the trees depending grow.

The teacher can make a selection of sentences from the reader or from other sources, if other or different sentences are required.

CHAPTER XII.

INFLECTION.

There are certain changes in the meaning or relation of words that are best expressed by a change in the form of the words.

Examples:—"boy" denotes one object,—"boys," more than one; "actor" names a male being,—"actress," a female being; "sweet" expresses simple quality,—"sweeter" expresses a comparison between two objects in respect of this quality; "he" denotes an object used as the principal part of the subject or predicate of thought,—"him" denotes the object of some attribute or relation.

This change in the form of the word to indicate a change in its meaning or relation is called INFLECTION.

Nouns may be inflected to denote, (1) more than one object,—Number; (2) to denote a female being,—Gender; (3) to denote a relation of possession,—Case.

Number.

Number is that grammatical attribute that denotes whether one or more than one object is meant. There are two numbers, the *Singular* and the *Plural*.

The Singular Number denotes that but one object is meant; as, *tree, man, boy*.

The Plural Number denoets that more than one object is meant; as *trees, men, boys*.

The Singular Number is denoted by the original and unmodified form of the noun.

The Plural Number is denoted in different ways, which gives rise to the following rules for forming plurals:

Rule I. To form the plural noun add *s* or *es* to the singular: as, ship-s, pace-s, box-es, glove-s, mass-es, boy-s.

NOTE.—*S* is added, (1) when euphony does not require an additional syllable: (2) when an additional syllable is required and the singular noun ends in a vowel. *Es* is added in other cases.

Rule II. Figures, letters, syllables, signs, symbols, etc., form their plurals by the addition of an apostrophe and the letter *s*; as 9's, +'s, *A*'s, *pro*'s, *y*'s.

Rule III. In compound words, and when two or more words are used to name the object, the plural sign is affixed to the word of leading significance; as, horse-*thieves,* brothers-in-law, the *brothers* Smith, *courts*-martial, *Knights* Templar.

EXCEPTIONS. 1. A few nouns form their plurals irregularly,—generally by some internal change in the word: as, *man, men; foot, feet; mouse, mice; ox, oxen.*

2. Nouns ending in *y preceded by a consonant* change *y* to *i* and add *es;* as, *fly, flies.*

3. A few nouns ending in *f* or *fe* change the *f* to *v* and add *s* or *es;* as, *beef, calf, wife, life, wolf,* etc.

4. Many nouns from other languages retain the plurals as in those languages: as, *axis, axes; focus, foci; basis, bases; datum, data.*

5. Nouns ending in *o* preceded by a consonant add *es* to form the plural:—except, *canto, octavo, quarto, zero, solo, tyro, halo, grotto,* and a few others.

NOTE.—Some nouns have the same form in both numbers;—as, *cattle, sheep, trout,* etc. Some have a plural form, but have either a singular or plural sense; as, *news, means, pains, riches, alms.*

Exercise.

Correct the misspelled words in the following and state the rule or exception violated:

Heros, dalies, shelfs, stratums, cantoes, monies, chimnies, folioes, twoes, foots, seraphims, pennies, potatoes, echoes, bodys, the brother Browns, son-in-laws, dwarves, flag-staves, loafs, beaus, memorandums, men-slayers, steps-son.

Construct sentences in which the plural forms of the following words shall be used:

Man, oats, grass, erratum, hypothesis, formula, oasis, focus, shears, sheep, fish, cattle, father-in-law.

CHAPTER XIII.

Gender.

Objects are classified according to sex into males, females, and objects having no sex. This gives rise to the grammatical attribute of GENDER.

The gender of names of the male sex is called the **Masculine Gender**; as, *father, boy, man.*

The gender of names of the female sex is called the **Feminine Gender**; as, *girl, mother, woman.*

The gender of names of objects without sex is called the **Neuter Gender**; as, *desk, tree, house.*

Many nouns name objects of either the male or female sex; as, *parent, child, clerk, merchant.* They are said to be of the **Common Gender.**

The Gender of nouns is distinguished in several ways:

1. By *inflection:* as, *actor, actress; host, hostess; executor, executrix; testator, testatrix; hero, heroine; Joseph, Josephine.*
2. By *different words:* as, *boy, girl; father, mother; man, woman.*
3. By *forming a compoud word*, one part of which indicates the sex; as, *man*-servant, *maid*-servant; *he*-goat, *she*-goat.

Exercise.

Write the feminine of the following words:

Nephew, negro, sir, duke, earl, gander, lad, director, prince, hero, lion, czar, beau, peer, drake, master, gentleman, landlord.

CHAPTER XIV.

Case.

Nouns may be inflected to denote the relation of possession; as, *John's* hat, *horse's* mettle, *ladies'* shoes. This inflection consists of the addition, either of the apostrophe and the letter *s*, or of the apostrophe only.

Objects may sustain the relation of subject of the thought, or of the object of some attribute; as, *John* struck *James:* but these relations are not expressed by inflection when *nouns* name the objects.

The distinction of nouns in respect of their relations to other parts of the sentence is called **Case.**

NOTE.—It will be seen that these relations are expressed in one of two ways; either by inflection or by the position of the words in the sentence. If, in the sentence, "*John struck James,*" the nouns change places, their relations are changed.

There are three Cases to correspond to the three classes of relations: viz., the *Nominative*, the *Possessive*, and the *Objective*.

The Nominative Case expresses the relation of subject or of non-attributive predicate: as, *John* studied his lesson; John is a good *boy*.

The Possessive Case expresses the relation of possession: as, the *boy's* book; the *man's* friend.

The Objective Case expresses the object of some attribute or relation: as, he saw *George* in the *town*.

NOTE.—The word *possession* as used in the definition above must not be understood to signify ownership, since the man does not own his friend. The word is used in a technical sense; all similar relations to those expressed in the examples given, being called in grammar *Possessive Relations*.

RULES FOR FORMING THE POSSESSIVE CASE.

Rule I. Singular nouns and plural nouns not ending in *s* add the apostrophe and the letter *s* to form the possessive case; plural nouns ending in *s* add the apostrophe only: as, *Charles's* book, *Burns's* poems, *boy's* class-room, *men's* hats.

NOTE—In a few cases only the apostrophe is added to singular nouns; as, conscience' sake, Moses' law. This is because the additional syllable would not sound well.

Rule II. In compound nouns the sign of possession is attached to the last word: as, the *Duke of Wellington's* sword, *Bowen & Stewart's* book-store, my *son-in-law's* house.

Exercise.

Correct the errors in the following:

A mothers' tenderness and a fathers care are natures gift's to mans' advantage. The portrait of her son's does not much resemble him.

Neither John nor his brother's opinion was regarded. Moses rod became a serpent. The judges decision was sustained. Robert Burns poems are popular. The shoe dealer sells men, and boys' boots, also ladies, misses, and childrens' shoes.

Write sentences using the possessive case of the following compound words:

Queen Victoria, John the carpenter, L. S. Ayres & Co., my brother George.

CHAPTER XV.

Person.

Objects must hold one of three relations to the speaker, viz.: as *speaking, spoken to,* or *spoken of.* This gives rise to PERSON in Grammar.

Person is that grammatical attribute that distinguishes the object as speaking, spoken to, or spoken of.

The First Person denotes the speaker.

The Second Person denotes the person spoken to.

The Third Person denotes the object spoken of.

The person of *nouns* is determined by the grammatical relation that they hold to other words in the sentence: as, John, come here,—second person; John came here,—third person; I, John, come,—first person.

Personal Pronouns.

There is a class of words whose original use in the language was to distinguish objects in their relations as *speaking, spoken to,* and *spoken of*; as, "I," denoting the speaker; "you," denoting the object spoken to; "he," "she," "it," denoting the object spoken of. These words are called Personal Pronouns.

LESSONS IN GRAMMAR.   51

Note.—While the person of nouns can only be determined by the grammatical relations that they hold to other words, the *person* of Personal Pronouns can always be determined by their *form*. The same is true in regard to *case*.

A Personal Pronoun is a word used to distinguish an object as speaker, person spoken to, or object spoken of.

There are five Personal Pronouns, viz.: "I," to denote the person speaking; "thou," or "you," to denote the person spoken to; and the masculine form "he," the feminine form "she," and the neuter form "it," to denote object spoken of.

These pronouns are inflected for case and number as follows:

FIRST PERSON.

	Singular.	Plural.
Nominative,	I,	We,
Possessive,	My, Mine,	Our, Ours,
Objective,	Me;	Us.

SECOND PERSON.

	Singular.	Plural.
Nominative,	Thou, You,	Ye, You,
Possessive,	Thy, Thine, Yours,	Your, Yours,
Objective,	Thee, You;	You.

THIRD PERSON.

	Singular.			Plural.
	Mas.	Fem.	Neut.	
Nominative,	He,	She,	It,	They,
Possessive,	His,	Her, Hers,	Its,	Their, Theirs,
Objective,	Him;	Her;	It;	Them.

Note.—Of the two forms given for the possessive, the longer is used when the noun which the pronoun limits is not expressed; as, the seats are *theirs*, not *yours*.

The Compound Personal Pronouns, *Myself*, plural, *Ourselves*; *Thyself*, plural, *Yourselves*; *Himself*, *Herself*, and *Itself*, with the common plural, *Themselves*, may each be either in the nominative or the objective case.

Exercise.

Correct the errors in the following sentences and give reasons:

John and me went to town. The book is yourn, not his', nor theirn. Their's is a sad case. They prostrated theirselves before the king. It is not her's but yourn. He spoke to John and I.

Relative and Interrogative Pronouns.

There is another class of Pronouns that perform the office of conjunctions: as, the man *that* I saw; God *who* created you. They are called Relative Pronouns.

A Relative Pronoun is a word that denotes an object previously mentioned and also performs the office of a conjunction.

The word to which the pronoun relates is called its **Antecedent.**

The Relative Pronouns are *who, which, what,* and *that.*

Who is inflected for case only, as follows: nom. *who*, poss. *whose*, obj. *whom*. The possessive of *which* is *whose.* The other relative pronouns have no inflection.

Who, which and *what* are often compounded with *ever* or *soever.* These compounds generally include both antecedent and relative.

What, as a relative pronoun, includes both antecedent and relative; as, "I know not what (that which) he says."

As is used as a relative after *such,* or *same*; e. g., such articles *as* I want.

But is used as a relative in sentences like the following: "There was not a man of them *but* shook with dread."

When is used as a relative in the following: "It is the hour *when* the nightingale's song is heard."

Where is a relative in the following: "This is the place *where* the house stood."

Whence and *whither* are sometimes used as relatives; e. g., "They knew not *whence* he came or *whither* he went."

Who and its compounds are applied to persons; *which* is applied to animals and things; *that* is applied to either persons or things.

That is generally used instead of *who* or *which*, when the clause that it introduces performs the office of a *Definitive Adjective*; as, He is the man *that* I saw. Bring me the book *that* is on the table.

Who or *which* is used when the clause is used as an *Epithet*; as, Our Father *who* art in Heaven. The sun *which* shines in the heavens.

Which sometimes refers to a whole sentence; as, I turned to the right, *which* led me astray.

Interrogative Pronouns.

When *who*, *which*, and *what*, are used in interrogative sentences to denote the object inquired for, they are called **Interrogative Pronouns.**

Which and *what* are also used as interrogative adjectives; as, *What* man? *Which* house?

Exercise.

Analyze the following sentences and parse the Relative Pronouns:

I venerate the man whose heart is warm. The fact that man's powers are limited, is not sufficiently recognized. The man that brought the letter was the carrier. The mail train which is generally so punctual, was late yesterday. The captain who is a man that I can trust, told me so yesterday. What did you come here for? It is in vain that you ask to escape. Health, which is precious to all, is invaluable to the poor. There is a sweetness in good verse which tickles even while it hurts.

> He that fights and runs away,
> May live to fight another day.

CHAPTER XVI.

ADJECTIVES.

Inflection.

Many adjectives are inflected to indicate that one or more objects are compared with one or more others in respect of some attribute.

This comparison may be made in two ways:

1. By comparing one part of any whole with other co-ordinate part or parts of the same whole: as, "John is *taller* than James." The two parts that make up the whole in this case are John and James; and the part John is compared with the part James in respect of height.

2. By comparing a part of any whole with that whole: as, the *tallest* tree in the garden. Here the whole is all the trees in the garden, and the part, a single tree, is compared with this whole.

The following sentence illustrates these two ways of comparing objects: "Solon was wise; wiser than any of his companions; the wisest man, in fact, of his time." The first clause expresses no comparison; the second expresses a comparison between Solon, a part, and companions, another part; the third expresses a comparison between Solon and all men living, including Solon; i. e., it compares a part with the whole.

The change in the form of the adjective to denote the different ways in which objects are compared is called **Comparison.**

The simple or uninflected form of the adjective is called the **Positive Form:** as, *good, tall, wise, large.*

The Comparative Form denotes that a comparison is made between two or more parts of a class, mass, or group of objects: as, *taller, better, wiser, larger.*

It is formed by adding *r* or *er*, or the prefix *more* or *less* to the positive: as, *happier, more happy, less happy.*

The Superlative Form denotes that a comparison is made between a part of a class of objects and the whole class; as, *tallest, best, wisest, largest.*

It is formed by adding *st* or *est,* or the prefix *most* or *least* to the positive: as, *happiest, most happy, least happy.*

NOTE.—Monosyllables and words accented on the last syllable are generally compared by adding *r* or *er* and *st* or *est.* Other adjectives are compared by the use of *more, most,* or *less, least.*

A few adjectives are compared irregularly: as, *bad, worse, worst; good, better, best; little, less, least; much, more, most,* etc.

Many adjectives do not admit of comparison: as, *this, that, such, superior, prior, minor, supreme, extreme, perfect, chief, final,* etc.

The *Demonstrative Adjectives, this* and *that,* are inflected for number: as, *these* men; *those* boys.

The *Numerals, other* and *another,* when used as nouns, are inflected for number and case: as, *others* may go; *another's* care.

Exercise.

Correct the errors in the following:

Most great abilities. Powerfulest man. The worser qualities. The hindest of the flock. The more junior of the sons. The greatest maximum of temperature. They were the greatest generals of any others in the army. Eve, the fairest of her daughters. The littlest was the amiablest. A more minor question. The extremest cold.

Analyze the following sentences and parse the adjectives; i. e., state all the grammatical properties and relations of each.

Point out the adjective phrases and clauses, and state the kind of attribute expressed by each:

King Arthur lived a blameless life in the good old times. Cæsar was the foremost man of all this world. Holy and heavenly thoughts shall consume her. Dryden, the poet, was one of the choice and master spirits of his age. Nimrod was a mighty hunter. Some pious drops the closing eye requires. The nearest and the remotest branches were loaded with fruit. He is the most powerful man of his company. The maximum of temperature was ninety-seven degrees.

ADVERBS.

Adverbs are inflected in the same manner as adjectives, to indicate comparison: as, *well, better, best; fast, faster, fastest.*

Most adverbs are compared by *more* and *most*: as, *swiftly, more swiftly, most swiftly.*

Exercise.

Point out the adverbs, the adverbial phrases, and the adverbial clauses in the following sentences, and state the kind of attribute expressed by each. Parse the adverbs:

America was discovered by Columbus in the year 1492. He sang as merrily as a lark on a spring morning. He performed his business cheerfully and with despatch. On the morrow he will leave me, as my hopes have flown before.

> Many a time and oft
> In the Rialto you have rated me.

> Idle, after dinner in his chair
> Sat a farmer, ruddy, fat, and fair.

CHAPTER XVII.

VERBS.

Sub-Classes.

We have learned (see page 18) that verbs are divided into two classes, viz.: Pure and Attributive.

Many attributive verbs that express action or relation require an immediate object to complete the predicate: as, he *struck* the ground; rain *moistens* the earth; he called *the dog, Carlo.*

Many other attributive verbs do not require the addition of an immediate object to complete the predicate: as, the sun *rises*; time *passes*; many *listened*; nations *rise* and *fall*.

This gives rise to the classification of attributive verbs into *Transitive* and *Intransitive.*

A Transitive Verb is one that requires an immediate object to complete the predicate.

An Intransitive Verb is one that does not require an immediate object to complete the predicate.

NOTE 1.—By *an immediate object* is meant, one that follows the verb without a preposition expressed or understood.

In the sentence, "He gave the book to me," *book* is the immediate or direct object, and *me* is called the remote or indirect object.

Intransitive as well as *transitive verbs* may have remote objects: as, the boy leaps upon the *horse*; here *horse* is the remote object of the intransitive verb *leaps*. The mark of distinction between these two classes of verbs is, that the transitive verb does not require a preposition to express the relation of the verb to the object, while the intransitive verb does.

NOTE 2.—An intransitive verb is sometimes used transitively, when it takes an immediate object that specifies the kind of action expressed by the verb; as, he *ran* a *race*; she *sang* a *song*; he *strikes* a *blow*.

In other words, the immediate object of an intransitive verb is always of kindred signification to the action expressed by the verb, while the immediate object of a transitive verb is not, but is something external to that action.

NOTE 3.—The different kinds of objects that verbs may have are as follows;

1. *Specifying object:* as, he gave a *gift.*
2. *Passive object:* as, she plucked the *rose.*
3. *Remote object:* as, I sold the horse to the *butcher.*
4. *Object of result:* as, he bought the horse *for service.*
5. *Factitive object:* as, they made him *bite the dust;* they made him *rich.*

The factitive object expresses the effect produced by the action expressed by the verb upon the immediate object.

Pure Verbs.—In addition to the verb *be*, which is always a *pure verb* except when it is used in the sense of *exist*, the verbs *seem, become, appear,* and some others are classed as pure verbs: as, he *seemed* a god; Wolsey *became* minister; John *appeared* mistaken.

CHAPTER XVIII.

Inflection of Verbs.

We have learned that verbs can be modified by words, phrases, and clauses. Verbs can also be modified by Inflection.

Verbs are modified by inflection:

1. To denote the direction of the action or relation as *to* or *from* the subject, called *Voice*:
2. To denote the *time* of the predicate, called *Tense*:
3. To denote the *mode* of the judging act, called *Mood*:
4. To denote the *number* and *person* of the subject.

Voice.

There are two *Voices*, the *Active* and the *Passive*.

The Active Voice denotes that the action or relation expressed by the verb proceeds from the subject: as, Mary *studies* her lesson; the horse *runs*; John *outran* James.

The Passive Voice denotes that the action or relation expressed by the verb is directed towards the subject: as, the house *was built* by the carpenter; the earth *is moistened* by the rain.

The object of the verb in the *active voice* becomes the subject when the verb is changed to the *passive voice*: as, the farmer sold *the ox*; *the ox* was sold by the farmer.

NOTE.—Since intransitive verbs can have no object they can have no *passive voice.*

Exercise.

Name the voice of each verb in the following sentences:

I am writing. He walked two miles. I besought him to go. The wind blew a hurricane. His friend was brought with him. He was caught by the storm. You will hit the mark. The hall had been swept by John. The prize was won by the soldier. They had not been better instructed. The ship was strained by the storm.

Tense.

In the sentence, " I *see* the sun," the time of the action is *now*, in the *present.* " I *saw* the sun," denotes that the action was in the *past.* " I shall see the sun," denotes that the action will be in the *future.* This change in the form of the verb to denote the time of the predicate, is called *Tense.*

Tense is that inflection of the verb that denotes the time of the predicate.

The time of every action must be either in the *present*, the *past*, or the *future*. A past action may be expressed as *related to the present*: as, I *have seen* you to-day; or, as *related to the past*: as, I *had seen* you yesterday. A future action may be expressed as related to the future: as, I *shall have seen* you by to-morrow.

The verb, therefore, may have *six tenses*: three *Absolute*, viz., *The Present, The Past,* and *The Future*; and three *Relative*, viz.., *The Present Perfect, The Past Perfect,* and *The Future Perfect.*

The Present Tense denotes the present time: as, I *see*.

The Past Tense denotes past time: as, I *saw*.

The Future Tense denotes future time: as, I *shall see.*

The Present Perfect Tense denotes past time related to the present: as, I *have seen* him to-day.

The Past Perfect Tense denotes past time related to the past: as, I *had seen* him yesterday.

The Future Perfect Tense denotes future time related to the future: as, I *shall have seen* him by to-morrow.

Exercise.

Name the tense of each verb in the following sentences :

John had swept the hall. The veterans led the attack. He won the prize. They will be sorry when they shall see what they have done. He had driven the cattle under the shed. We had not gone far before it began to rain. They drank too freely of iced water. No one has begun. The storm will have caught him before he leaves the forest.

Mood.

We have seen that a modifier of the copula of thought, or the judging act, may be expressed by words, phrases, and clauses : as, he will *probably* go; *if he refuse*, I will go. A modification of the judging act may also be expressed by inflection.

When the judgment is unmodified, or when the modification is expressed by another word, phrase, or clause, the verb is said to be in the *Indicative Mood*: as, the horse *runs*; he *will* probably·*go*; he *will be* successful if he be honest.

The verb is sometimes modified to denote that the judgment is a *necessary one* : as, two and two *must be* four. This modification is expressed by the auxiliary verb *must*.

This inflection of the verb is called the *Necessary Mood*.

NOTE.—A similar modification of the judgment is expressed by the modal, *necessarily*, when used to modify a word in the indicative mood: as, two and two are *necessarily* four.

When the judgment is represented as possible but not certain, or as dependent upon that which is unknown or impossible, it is called a *contingent* judgment: as, he *may go*, but I think it doubtful; *should* he *go* I will inform you; if he *be* honest he will be successful; *were* I you I *would* not *go*; although he *slay* me, I will trust in him.

Contingency is expressed by the words *may, can, might, could, would, should, be, were,* and by the uninflected form of some tenses.

The inflection of the verb to denote that the judgment is *contingent* is called the *Potential* or *Contingent Mood*.

NOTE.—The name *contingent* is more appropriate for this mood, but since the name *potential* is in common use it is probably best to employ it. It will be seen, however, that its meaning should be extended to embrace those forms commonly classed under the *Subjunctive Mood*.

The judgment may be modified to denote *peremptory will*, or *strong desire*: as, *begone*, thou villian; *come* quickly, I beseech you.

This form of the verb is called the *Imperative Mood*.

The Indicative Mood denotes that the judgment is unmodified.

The Necessary Mood denotes that the judgment is a necessary one.

The Potential Mood denotes that the judgment is contingent.

The Imperative Mood denotes that the judgment is modified by peremptory will or strong desire.

Infinitives.

In the sentence, "To walk is better than to run," *to walk* and *to run* are commonly called verbs in the infinitive mood. They are not verbs, since they do not express a relation discerned between a subject and predicate of thought. They are more properly nouns, since they are used to name actions.

Since *Infinitives* may express action, they may be modified by an object, like a verb: as, to speak *the truth* is well; to act *the truth* is better.

Infinitives are sometimes used as adjectives: as, time *to come* is called future.

An infinitive may sometimes have a subject: as, it is wrong for *him to act* thus. The subject of an infinitive is always in the objective case.

Participles.

A *Participle* is a word derived from a verb, and used:

1. To assist in forming the different tenses of the verb: as, I have *seen*; I am *talking*; he had *gone*.

2. To denote an object of thought, or some modification of an

object: as, *walking* is better than *riding*; an *advancing* army; a star *seen* through the cloud.

Participles like infinitives may be modified by objects: as, I left him studying *his lesson.*

A participle may sometimes have a subject; "*He consenting*, I will be present."

There are two participles, called *the present*, and *the past*: as, *seeing, seen.*

Exercise.

(a). Name the mood of each verb in the following sentences:

(b). Point out the infinitives and the participles, and name the part of speech for which each is used.

To spare thee now is past my power. You like to hear from me. He made them give up the spoils. He felt the pangs of dying enter his soul. You must not attempt to envelop your ideas, or polish your taste, or refine your sentiments. May that blessing ever last. A man might have all these qualities and yet not be perfect. I would therefore exhort you earnestly. She could not be beguiled. By my being kind to him, I have his confidence.

CHAPTER XIX.

Conjugation of the Verb.

A regular arrangement of all the different forms of the verb is called *Conjugation.*

To make these different forms we use:

1. The present and the past tenses of the verb;

2. The present and past participles;

3. The auxiliary verbs: *must; may, might; can, could; shall, should; will, would; have, had; do, did; be, was, were, been.*

The Principal Parts of a verb are, the simplest forms of the *present* and *past tenses,* the *present participle,* and the *past participle.*

NOTE.—They are called the Principal Parts because some one of them is the is the chief part of each form.

Regular Verbs are those that form their *past tense* and *past participle* by adding *ed* to the present: as, present, I *love;* past, I *loved;* past participle, I *have loved.*

Other verbs are called *Irregular*: as, I *see,* I *saw,* I *have seen.*

Irregular Conjugation.

To Be.

Present.	Past.	Present Participle.	Past Participle.
Be.	Was.	Being.	Been.

Indicative Mood.

PRESENT TENSE.

Singular.
1st Person, I am,
2d Person, { You are, Thou art,
3d Person, He is;

Plural.
1. We are,
2. You are,
3. They are.

PAST TENSE.

Singular.
1. I was,
2. { You were, Thou wast,
3. He was;

Plural.
1. We were,
2. You were,
3. They were.

FUTURE TENSE.

Singular.
1. I shall be,
2. { You will be, Thou wilt be,
3. He will be;

Plural.
1. We shall be,
2. You will be,
3. They will be.

When determination is to be expressed as well as future time, the following forms are used for the *future tense:*

Singular.
1. I will be,
2. { You shall be,
   { Thou shalt be,
3. He shall be;

Plural.
1. We will be,
2. You shall be,
3. They shall be.

PRESENT PERFECT.

Singular.
1. I have been,
2. { You have been.
   { Thou hast been,
3. He has been;

Plural.
1. We have been,
2. You have been.
3. They have been.

PAST PERFECT.

Singular.
1. I had been,
2. { You had been,
   { Thou hadst been,
3. He had been;

Plural.
1. We had been,
2. You had been,
3. They had been.

FUTURE PERFECT.

Singular.
1. I shall or will have been,
2. { You will or shall have been,
   { Thou wilt or shalt have been,
3. He will or shall have been;

Plural.
1. We shall or will have been,
2. You will or shall have been,
3. He will or shall have been.

Necessary Mood.

PRESENT TENSE.

Singular.
1. I must be,
2. { You must be,
   { Thou must be,
3. He must be;

Plural.
1. We must be,
2. You must be,
3. They must be.

PRESENT PERFECT.

Singular.
1. I must have been,
2. You or thou must have been,
3. He must have been;

Plural.
1. We must have been,
2. You must have been,
3. They must have been.

Potential Mood.

PRESENT TENSE.

Singular.
1. I may or can be,
2. { You may or can be,
   { Thou mayst or canst be,
3. He may or can be;

Plural.
1. We may or can be,
2. You may or can be,
3. They may or can be,

LESSONS IN GRAMMAR.

Another form of this tense is as follows:

	Singular.		Plural.
1.	I be,	1.	We be,
2.	{ You be, Thou be,	2.	You be,
3.	He be;	3.	They be.

PAST TENSE.

Singular.
1. I might, could, would, or should be,
2. { You might, could, would, or should be, Thou mightst, couldst, wouldst, or shouldst be,
3. He might, could, would, or should be;

Plural.
1. We might, could, would, or should be,
2. You might, could, would, or should be,
3. They might, could, would, or should be.

Another form of this tense is as follows:

	Singular.		Plural.
1.	I were,	1.	We were,
2.	{ You were, Thou wert,	2.	You were,
3.	He were;	3.	They were.

PRESENT PERFECT.

	Singular.		Plural.
1.	I may or can have been,	1.	We may or can have been,
2.	{ You may or can have been, Thou mayst or canst have been,	2.	You may or can have been,
3.	He may or can have been,	3.	They may or can have been,

PAST PERFECT.

Singular.
1. I might, could, would, or should have been,
2. { You might, could, would, or should have been, Thou mightst, couldst, wouldst, or shouldst have been,
3. He might, could, would, or should have been;

Plural.
1. We might, could, would, or should have been,
2. You might, could, would, or should have been,
3. They might, could, would, or should have been.

Note.—The definitions heretofore given of the different tenses apply only to the tenses of the indicative mood. For the sake of convenience the same names are given to the other verb forms.

Imperative Mood.

PRESENT TENSE.

Singular. Plural.
2. Be (thou or you). 2. Be (ye or you).

Infinitives.

Present, *to be*; perfect, *to have been.*

Participles.

Present, *being*, past, *been*; perfect, *having been.*

The following are the *tense forms* in the first person, of the irregular verb *to see*, in both the *active* and the *passive voice:*

ACTIVE VOICE.		PASSIVE VOICE.
	Present Tense.	
I see.		I am seen.
	Past Tense.	
I saw.		I was seen.
	Future Tense.	
I shall see.		I shall be seen.
	Present Perfect.	
I have seen.		I have been seen.
	Past Perfect.	
I had seen.		I had been seen.
	Future Perfect.	
I shall see.		I shall be seen.

Potential Mood.

Present Tense.

I may or can see.   I may or can be seen.

Past Tense.

I might, could, would, or should see.   I might, could, would, or should be seen.

Present Perfect.

I may or can have seen.   I may or can have been seen.

Past Perfect.

I might, could, etc. have seen.   I might, could, etc. have been seen.

Another way of expressing contingency is by the use of the uninflected forms of the different tenses: as,

Singular.	*Plural.*
1. I see,	1. We see,
2. Thou or you see,	2. You see,
3. He see;	3. They see.

Example: If he see him, he will inform him.

Imperative Mood.

Present Tense.

2. See.   2. Be seen.

NOTE.—Other forms are sometimes borrowed to express command or strong desire: as, thou *shall* not *kill*; *may* Heaven *bless* you!

Infinitives.

Present.

To see.   To be seen.

Perfect.

To have seen.   To have been seen.

Participles.

Present.

Seeing.   Being seen.

Past.

Seen.   ———

Perfect.

Having seen.   Having been seen.

Continuous Tenses.

To denote *continuous time*, some form of the auxiliary verb *be*, and the present participle are employed: as, *I am reading, I was reading, I have been reading, I shall have been reading, I may be reading*, etc.

In a few verbs some of the tenses are wanting: *ought* has but two tenses, the *present* and the *past;* *beware* is used in but few of the tenses. Such verbs are called *Defective Verbs.*

The conjugation of the *regular verb* is in every respect similar to that of the *irregular verb.*

To determine whether a verb is regular or irregular, teachers and pupils are referred to the dictionary.

Exercise.

Name the *voice, mood, tense, person* and *number* of each verb in the following sentences:

I am writing. He walked two miles. They drank water too freely. We had not gone before it began to rain. You will have seen him before I return. The boys have learned their lessons. I shall not go to day. They durst not betray him. He abides in town. His friend was induced to go. She has just completed her work. John had finished reading before I entered. I shall drown; nobody will help me. To spare thee now is past my power. Though the event is possible it is hardly probable. I know not if it be so. I feared lest they should arrive and find us unprepared. It is and must be true. He may have erred. He that is his own foe will assuredly be destroyed. By suffering we may possibly avoid sinning; but by sinning we certainly can not avoid suffering. If Luther had been born in the tenth century, he would have effected no reformation. We may die, it may be, ignominiously and on the scaffold. Would you listen to conscience, it would tell you whether you really do as you would be done by. Were you omniscient you might be allowed to rule. Had he gone farther he might have fared worse. Whether he confess or not, the truth will certainly be discovered.

Analyze the above sentences.

Correct the errors in the forms of the verbs in the following sentences:

He has abided here a long time. They begun wrong. They blowed the trumpet long and loud. The police brung him to the station. She had catched cold. They come home an hour ago. He done the job yesterday. They drunk no cider. The boy had ate green apples and had fell sick. The stream was froze over. The vessel laid in the harbor. I had never saw such a sight before. I seen him do it. The man had stole two watches. She has spoke but once. He had come some hours before. If he is honest he will be successful. If I was you, I would not do it. Although he slays me yet will I trust in him. I will be drownded; nobody shall help me.

CHAPTER XX.

SYNTAX.—CONSTRUCTION OF SENTENCES.

Concord.

The following rules should be observed in the construction of sentences:

RULE I.—The subject of a verb is put in the *nominative case.*

RULE II.—The subject of an infinitive is put in the objective case: as, "For *him* to act thus is ungrateful."

NOTE.—The particle *for* in this sentence is an expletive used to introduce the sentence.

RULE III.—The subject of a participle used as a noun is in the possessive case: as, "I objected to *his* going."

RULE IV.—A noun or pronoun used as a predicate is put in the same case as the subject: as, "The men were *they* whom I saw;" "I knew it to be *him.*"

NOTE.—In the last sentence, "it to him," is an infinitive clause of which *it* is the subject and *him* is the predicate.

Rule V.—A verb must be in the same number and person as the subject: as, "*Thou art* the man."

Notes.—1. When the same predicate is affirmed of two or more different subjects connected by *and*, the verb is in the plural number: as, John and James *are* here.

2. If but one object is meant, the verb is in the singular: as, the great statesman and orator is dead; the wheel and axle is a mechanical power.

3. When two or more singular subjects are taken distributively, the verb is in the singular number: as, each man, woman, and child has something to do.

4. When a collective noun is the subject, the verb is singular if the group or collection is viewed as a unit; if reference is made to the individuals composing the collection, the verb is plural: as, the congregation was large; the assembly were divided in their opinions.

5. When two or more subjects are connected by disjunctive conjunctives, the verb takes the number of the nearest: as, neither the boys, nor the girls, nor the teacher *was* present.

6. In other cases the leading subject in the thought determines the number and person of the verb: as, *they* as well as I *are* interested.

Rule VI.—Pronouns must agree with their antecedents in person, gender, and number.

Notes.—1. If the antecedents are of different persons, the pronoun agrees with the first person rather than the second or third, and with the second rather than the third.

2. When there are two or more antecedents connected by conjunctions, the number and person of the pronoun are determined by principles similar to those that determine the number and person of the verb having two or more subjects.

Rule VII.—Appositives are put in the same case as the words that they modify: as, "The earth is the Lord's—*his* who made it."

Rule VIII.—Words used to denote objects addressed, are put in the nominative case: as, "Lift up your heads, O *ye* gates."

Note.—When a pronoun of the first person is thus used, it is put in the objective case: as, "O miserable *me*."

Rule IX.—Words denoting the object of an action or relation are put in the objective case: as, "John gave *him* to *me*."

Rule X.—The subject of an abstract is expressed by a noun or pronoun in the possessive case: as, "*Mary's* faithfulness was the cause of *her* delaying the messenger."

Note.—To denote the relation of possession between two concrete objects, the possessive case is also used; as, "Mary's cousin;" "The Czar of Russia's palace."

2. If the possessive phrase is composed of two or more nouns relating *to the same object*, the sign of possession is annexed to the last: as, "Mary, John, and Henry's father;" but if they relate *to different objects* the possessive sign is annexed to each: as, "Mary's, John's, and Henry's father." In this phrase, Mary, John, and Henry are represented as having different fathers.

3. In the phrase, "The house of Mr. Stanton's," the particle *of* simply denotes identity; the expression is equivalent to "the house, namely, Mr. Stanton's." It does not mean the house of Mr. Stanton's houses.

RULE XI.—The tenses of the principal and subordinate verbs should be in harmony with each other, and with the time expressed by the other parts of the sentence; as, "He *affirmed* that he *would go* to-morrow."

The following sentences are, therefore, incorrect:

I *have been* sick yesterday. If this should be done I *will* at once *withdraw*. He hid himself least he *shall be impressed*. I intended *to have gone* immediately. I intended *to go* the day before.

RULE XII.—In compound sentences, like forms should be used in all the parts; as, "He *stoppeth* not to consider his way, but *presseth* on to ruin."

Exercise.

Correct the errors in the following sentences and state the rule violated:

We was glad. You was there. He dare not do it. John or I is to go. The congregation were large. The Acts of the Apostles were written. Whom did he think was absent? By me being kind to him I won his confidence. Them that be wise shall be happy. They traveled as fast as him. He protested against them embarking in the enterprise. The party were brilliant. The audience was gratified. The man or his friends is to blame. The committee were divided in its sentiments. You who was present, are able to speak. Let every one esteem others better than themselves. One or the other will give their opinion. He is like a beast of prey who destroys without pity. Nero, who is a name for cruelty. Thou art my friend, else would I reprove you. Do you know who you are speaking to? He did not know who to suspect. By observing of truth you will become wise. He spoke of Job, he who was so patient. They imprisoned Columbus, he who discovered a continent. After I visited France I returned to England. He was absent this entire week. The day has not been so pleasant as I expected it to have been. He said he is in great haste. He professed to be very studious the day before; but admitted that he has been very negligent yesterday. He will take due heed lest he falls. I told him that I will do it. He is so sensible of his guilt that he dare not reply. Although he slays me, yet I will trust in him. Though he write well, he can not read it. Was he ever so great, such conduct would debase him.

CHAPTER XXI.

ANALYSIS OF SENTENCES.

Subject, Predicate, and Copula.

We have learned that every sentence contains three elements, viz., the subject, the predicate, and the copula.

The Subject of a sentence denotes that of which something is affirmed: it must, therefore, express an object of thought, and is either a noun or pronoun, or some word, phrase, or clause used substantively; i. e., as a noun.

The Predicate of a sentence denotes that which is affirmed of the subject, and must, therefore, express some object of thought, or an attribute of some object.

When a predicate denotes an object, it is called a *non-attributive predicate*; when it denotes an attribute, it is called an *attributive predicate*: as, "the boy is *a student;*" "the boy *writes;*" "the boy is *studious.*"

The predicate may, therefore, be expressed by a *noun* or *pronoun*, an *adjective*, or an *attributive verb*.

The Copula is the element of the sentence that expresses the relation which the mind discerns between the subject and the predicate of thought.

NOTE.—Objects and attributes may exist independent of the mind; but it is not until the mind discerns some relation existing between them, that a thought can come into being. Hence this action of the mind is a vital element of the thought, and the word expressing this activity is an important element in the sentence. In the sentence, "The boy is studious," *is* denotes that the mind discerns that one of the attributes of the boy is persistence in study. In the sentence, "The boy writes," the copula and the predicate are combined in the verb *writes*.

Grammatical and Logical Elements.

Each element of the sentence may consist of several words: as, "The fairest way of conducting a dispute is, probably, to exhibit one by one the arguments of your opponents." In this sentence, the entire subject is expressed by the words, "the fairest way of conducting a dispute;" the thought-predicate, by the words, "to exhibit one by one the arguments of your opponents;" the judging act, by "is probably."

Each of these elements has a principal and a modifying part; as, "way," the principal part of the subject; "is," of the copula; and "to exhibit," of the predicate.

The principal part of each element is called the *grammatical* element; the principal part together with its modifying words, is called the *logical* element.

Exercise.

Point out the *grammatical* and *logical* elements of the sentences in preceding exercises.

Grammatical Subject.

The *grammatical subject* may be:

1. A noun or some word used as a noun: as, "The *good* are respected."

2. Letters, symbols, signs, etc.: as, "The ✕'s and the +'s resemble each other."

3. An infinitive or participle: as, "*To steal* is base." "*Telling* stories is pleasant entertainment."

4. A substantive clause: as, "*That he should act thus* is unfortunate."

Grammatical Predicate.

The *grammatical predicate* may be:

1. An attributive verb: as, "The horse *runs* rapidly."

2. An adjective, or a phrase or clause used to express some attribute of the subject: as, "The apple is *sweet.*" He seems *to act* honestly."

3. A noun, or a substantive word, phrase, or clause: as, "It is he;" "His duty is *to go;*" "The objection is *that he is not honest.*"

Grammatical Copula.

The *grammatical copula* may be:

1. The pure verb *to be*: as, "Sugar *is* sweet."

2. The copulative verbs *become, seem, appear, consists of, equals, is composed of,* and the like: as, "Water *is composed of* oxygen and hydrogen." "Great Britain *consists of* England, Scotland, and Wales."

3. It may be combined with the predicate, forming an attributive verb: as, "John *reads* well."

Modifiers.

The subject, or any word used to express an object of thought, may be modified by an adjective, or by any word, phrase, or clause used as an adjective.

An attributive predicate, or any word used to express an attribute may be modified by an adverb, or by any word, phrase, or clause used as an adverb.

NOTE.—The words *here, there, yonder, now, then,* and others denoting relations to space or to time, are generally classed as adverbs. They are frequently used in the predicate to express an attribute of the subject: as, "The man is here." When thus used they are properly predicate adjectives. The mark of an adverb is that it expresses an attribute of another attribute: as, "The horse runs rapidly." In this sentence "rapidly" expresses the quality of the attribute expressed by the verb.

A word expressing an attribute of action or of relation, may be modified by a word, phrase or clause used to express the object of the attribute: as, " He strikes *the ground;*" "To speak *the truth* is well;" "He said *that he would remain;*" "Deserving *success,* he obtained it."

The copula may be modified by a modal, or by any word, phrase, or clause use as a modal: as, " He will *probably* go;" " He will *of necessity* go;" " He will go *if it be possible.*"

Modal modifiers are of three classes:

1. Those that indicate the character of the assertion, in respect of its quality or degree: as, " He will *certainly* come;" " He would *not* act just as you have described;" "A is greater than B; *much more* is C greater than B;" " I will trust in him *although he slay me;*" "The truth will be discovered *whether he confess or not.*"

2. Those that indicate contingency of the asserting or judging act: as, " He will *possibly* come;" " He will come *if he be informed;*" "Our opinion, *such a state of things being supposed,* would be very different."

NOTE.—The copula modifier in the last sentence is an *abridged clause.* It is equivalent to, " if such a state of things be supposed." The subject of the participle in such clauses is said to be used *independently* or *absolutely* with the participle.

3. Those that denote that the judgment is a necessary one: as, " He *of necessity* remains weak, who takes no exercise."

Exercise.

Analyze the following sentences:

(An order and modal for the analysis of a sentence will be found on pages 41, 42 and 43.)

Amid the roses, fierce Repentance wears her snaky crest. His purpose is to avert bad consequences.

> Leaves have their time to fall,
> And flowers to wither at the north wind's breath.

Now, therefore, let thy servant abide in place of the lad, a bondman to my lord.

> With droll sobriety they raised a smile
> At Folly's cost, themselves unmoved the while.

Collecting, classifying, contrasting, and weighing facts, are processes made use of in teaching method.

> The boy stood on the burning deck,
> Whence all but him had fled.

The rose that all are praising, is not the rose for me.

How France was saved from this great humiliation, and how the great alliance was preserved, will now be seen.

> She loved me for the dangers I had passed,
> And I loved her that she did pity them.

Disquieted by imaginary alarms, insensible to the danger that awaits them, people are taught to court that servitude which will be the source of misery to themselves and to posterity. Go into Turkey, where the Pachas will tell you that the Turkish government is the most perfect in the world. All that he does is to distribute what others produce; which is the least part of the business.

> Here Cumberland lies, having acted his parts,
> The Terence of England, the mender of hearts;
> A flattering painter, who made it his care
> To draw men as they ought to be, not as they are.

"Alas!" replied the adventurer, "I must submit to the conditions of my enterprise." If we had to walk a hundred miles, we should still have to set but one foot at a time. Return with him, young reader, if thou be walking in the same downward path, lest his dream become thy reality.

PART II.

A COURSE IN COMPOSITION.

CHAPTER I.

Relations of Reading and Grammar to Composition.

1. The results to be gained through the study of Grammar are two-fold:

1. The student is taught to interpret the thoughts of others, as expressed on the printed page, by a thorough study of the influence of word, phrase, and clause, and of inflection, in expressing the different modifications of thought.

2. By learning the use of these different modifications, in expressing the thoughts of others, he learns to apply this knowledge in the expression of his own thoughts.

Primarily, then, the study of Grammar is the study of the constructed sentence, for the purpose of learning to interpret the thought expressed by it. The secondary object is not less important, but holds a subordinate place in the teaching of technical grammar.

2. In the study of composition the object is also two-fold:

1. To teach the student how to think upon any subject; how to collect and arrange the material of his thought with method, and thus produce clearness of thought.

2. To learn to express his thought so that it shall be clear to others.

Primarily, then, the study of composition has for its object, training the mind to collect, select, and arrange thoughts. The second object is of equal importance, since it is only through continued practice in the accurate expression of thought, that we can learn to think accurately.

Thus it may be seen, that, while grammar and composition differ in their primary objects, their secondary objects are practically the same. Nor do the primary objects differ so widely as the above statements imply; since, by the study of the thoughts of others, as expressed in the sentence and in connected discourse, the student learns how to collect and arrange original thoughts in regard to any given subject.

3. The primary object in teaching children to read is to give them the power to obtain thoughts from the printed page. This we have said is also the leading object of grammar teaching. Reading and grammar may, therefore, be considered as co-ordinate subjects in this particular. The secondary object in the reading lesson is to acquire a distinct enunciation and a correct pronunciation of words, and a natural and appropriate modulation of the voice. The common error is to make these secondary objects the primary ones, and rely upon the recitation in grammar to give the instruction necessary for a correct interpretation of the thought.

The true view seems to be to consider reading, spelling, grammar, and composition as holding such intimate mutual relations, that each should be taught "in the presence" of the others. And of such paramount importance are the results sought by the study of language, both to the culture of the individual, and to his varied relations to others, that in every period of the pupil's school life, this study should have a prominent place.

The following pages are designed to suggest a practical method for conducting the study of grammar and composition in the different grades of our public schools.

CHAPTER II.

First and Second Year Grades.

The instruction in language in this grade should have for its object:

1. To teach the names of objects, and attributes, and to call these words at sight.

2. To practice the pupil in the oral expression of his thoughts about an object.

3. To teach him, by continued practice, the proper form of verb, pronoun, adjective, etc., to be used in different sentences.

4. To teach him to write sentences from dictation.

5. To teach him to interpret the thoughts expressed by the sentences in the reader.

6. To teach him to spell correctly all the words that he uses.

Much of this instruction is given in the reading lesson. There are other portions of it that can be best given in separate exercises. Conversation lessons should be given daily, in which the pupils should be taught:

1. The plurals of irregular nouns;
2. The form of the personal pronouns when used, (1) as subject, (2) as predicate, (3) as object;
3. The proper form of the irregular verbs in common use in the the past, present perfect, and past perfect tenses;
4. The correct use of *a* and *an*;
5. The proper form of the verb having a singular or a plural subject;
6. The correct use of *these, those,* and *them*;
7. The correct use of the interrogatives, *who* and *whom*;
8. The proper form for adjectives and adverbs;
9. The correct use of *as* and *like.*

This instruction should be given by leading the child to use the words in answering questions, and then correcting his mistakes. Any formal statement of rules should be avoided, the teacher relying on continued and persistent practice for fixing the proper form in the pupil's mind.

7. In the second year much practice should be given in writing sentences, both original and from dictation.

8. The pupils should be taught a few choice selections of prose and poetry, which should be frequently repeated before the school.

CHAPTER III.

Third Year Grade.

The pupils in this grade, in addition to the usual instruction in reading and spelling, should have a daily exercise in either written or oral composition. The exercises may consist of:

1. Naming the parts of objects.

2. Oral description of objects, the child composing the sentences that make up the description, in answer to questions asked by the teacher. The teacher should pursue a methodical course in questioning upon every subject. The different objects in the school-room, especially pictures, make excellent themes.

In studying a picture the teacher should question in regard to, (1) position; (2) form and size; (3) kind; (4) objects represented in fore-ground, in back-ground; (5) story suggested by the picture.

3. Pupils should be led to study objects at home, and describe them from memory, in school; the teacher directing their study.

The following is an illustration of a plan that may be pursued:

Theme: OUR CAT.

(1). State color and size.
(2). Name the parts.
(3). Describe the teeth.

(4). Describe the feet, stating the number of toes and arrangement of claws.

(5). Describe the eyes.

(6). State habits.

(7). Relate some anecdote.

4. Constant attention should be given, in every recitation, to the correct use of words in sentences. (See directions for first and second year grades.)

5. Pupils should complete at least one written exercise each week.

The following method is suggested for developing a composition in this grade:

Suppose that the pupil has been studying the eye of the cat, and has learned that in color it is a greenish yellow, having in the middle part a narrow black stripe running up and down. The teacher has suggested to him to examine the size of this black stripe in the day time, and in the evening, and he has found it to be much larger in the evening. He has been told the reason of this, and has learned how the cat can see in the dark. All of the information required should be obtained, before the writing exercise is commenced. The teacher may then proceed as follows:

(1). Ask where the eye is located, and how protected from injury.

. Answers to these questions given by one pupil, and corrected and improved by the others, will form the first sentences in the composition, which should be written upon the blackboard by the teacher as dictated by the pupils.

(2). Question as to form and color of the eye, and write as before.

(3). Question as to position, form, and size of the pupil of the eye. Write.

(4). Question as to use and adaptation of the pupil of the eye. Write.

(5). Question as to use of the eye. Write.

The composition thus produced will be the result of the combined efforts of the school; the teacher simply directing their thought, and deciding when each sentence is in the proper form for use. The pupils should also dictate the spelling, capitals, and punctuation. The composition thus completed should be copied by each pupil. Later in the grade the teacher need only have the sentences stated, and require each pupil to write from dictation. It is believed that in this grade it is best that the compositions be all developed in this way, and that they all be uniform;—the product of the entire school.

6. Pupils in this grade should be taught to observe the use of capitals, punctuation marks, plural and possessive case forms, and to discover the rule for their use. They should learn:

(1). That every sentence, every line of poetry, every proper name, and the words I and O, begin with capitals.

(2). They should discover that the apostrophe is used to show the omission of letters or words: as, *e'er* for *ever*, *o'clock* for *of the clock*, *don't* for *do not*, etc. They should also be taught the use of the apostrophe to indicate possession.

7. Sentences should be distinguished as *statements*, *questions*, *commands*, and *exclamations*, and the closing mark of punctuation for each should be taught.

8. A few carefully chosen selections in prose and poetry, should be learned by the school, and frequently repeated by different pupils.

9. Every error in the use of words in each school exercise should be corrected, the pupil being required to repeat the sentence, using the correct form.

10. Pupils should occasionally be called upon to re-produce in writing their general lesson, or some short story or sketch, read by the teacher.

CHAPTER IV.

Fourth Year Grade.

1. Pupils in this grade should observe the rules for plurals, capitals, punctuation, etc., learned in the preceding grades. They should learn in addition:

1. The rules for plurals, when the singular noun ends in *y*, and when it is a compound word. Irregular plurals should be taught.

2. The use of the comma, (1) when a noun is used in direct address; (2) where there is a succession of several co-ordinate words or phrases; (3) where the order of the principal elements of the sentence is transposed.

3. The use of the period in abbreviations.

2. The work in composition commenced in the preceding grades should be extended to include:

1. A written description of objects from an outline prepared by the school. Instead of developing the entire composition, as in the preceding grade, only the outline of it should be developed in the order in which the theme is to be discussed, and written upon the black-board. The pupil should copy this outline, which should be followed by his composition. This he should write without any further assistance from the teacher, except that she should help him to determine the correct orthography of words, and questions in the construction of sentences about which he may be ignorant. Before beginning to write, the teacher should know that the pupil has the necessary information. The theme should have been assigned two or more days before, and the pupil instructed how and where to find this information. It should then be discussed by the school, and each pupil be called upon to tell what he has learned. The teacher may then make such additions to this stock of knowledge as seem necessary. The pupils are now prepared to write, but not before.

The following outlines may be suggestive:

My Desk.
{
1. Position.
2. Size and form.
3. The parts and their uses.
4. Design.
5. Adaptation to design.
}

{
Seat.
Back.
Top.
Shelf.
Legs.
}

The Camel.
1. Where found.
2. Size, form, color.
3. Description of parts, and adaptation to country, climate, etc.
   - Head.
   - Neck.
   - Body.
   - Feet.
   - Legs.
4. Habits of life.
5. Intelligence, disposition, etc.
6. Anecdote illustrating the same.
7. Use to man.

NOTE.—The second outline is fuller than most pupils of this grade can complete, but since description is one of the divisions of discourse, studied in all the grades, this complete analysis is given here to avoid repetition.

3. Pictures should be described, and stories written which the pictures suggest. No assistance should be given, other than general directions, in the composition of the story. It is intended as an exercise of the imagination, and the child should be left perfectly free.

4. The pupils of this grade should be taught to write letters of friendship. The name and place of the different parts of the letter should be learned, viz.:

1. *Heading;* consisting of place and date. 2. *Introduction;* consisting of the address and salutation. 3. *Body* of the letter. 4. *Conclusion;* consisting of complimentary close and signature.

NOTE.—In letters of friendship the address may be placed at the close, opposite or a little below the signature.

The following is an appropriate form for a social letter:

Indianapolis, Ind.,
Feb. 4, 1877.

My Dear Brother,

_____

_____

_____

Mr. Henry Smith,   *Your loving sister,*
    Dayton, Ohio.   *Mary Smith.*

The following is an appropriate form for a superscription :

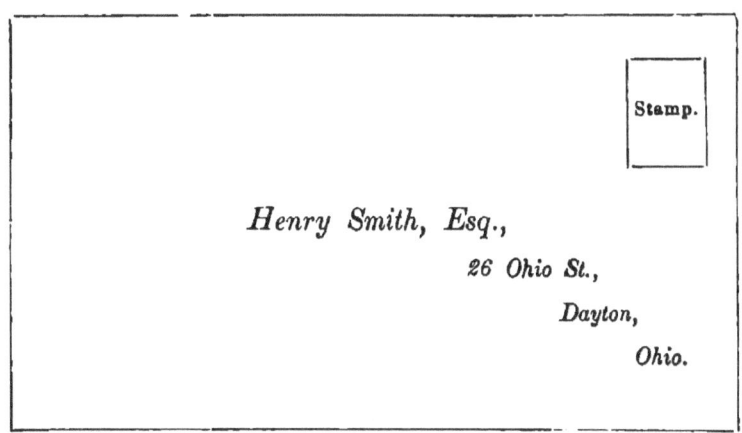

Letters of friendship should be written in a conversational style, and be free from all ostentation. They should contain such matter as will interest the person to whom they are written, and should not dwell upon the writers troubles and grievances, nor his personal affairs, except so far as these are matters of interest to the receiver of the letter.

In teaching this subject, the teacher should lead the pupils to arrange their topics in proper order, and to complete one topic before commencing another. This should not be carried so far, however, as to make the letter appear studied and unnatural. What one should *write* to a friend is what he would *say* to him, if he were present.

NOTE.—Teachers will fine much valuable information in a little book, entitled, *How to Write Letters*, published by Sower, Potts & Co., Philadelphia.

5. Pupils should be required to write abstracts of lessons. This exercise should occasionally take the place of the regular recitation, and be a written review or recitation upon some topic in geography or natural science.

7. All errors in the use of language in every recitation should be corrected, the pupil being constantly trained to talk correctly.

8. Carefully selected poems and descriptions in prose should be learned and frequently recited before the school, as suggested in the work of the preceding grades.

9. Pupils should be taught how to fold letters to put in envelopes, and how to fold and file papers.

CHAPTER V.

Fifth Year Grade.

1. Pupils in this grade should learn in the reading class, as a help in determining the thought, to point out the principal and modifying parts of the subjects and predicates of the sentences read. This is the beginning of the instruction in grammar, as a distinctive subject of study. No attempt should be made to do more than teach the child to determine the grammatical and logical predicate and subject of any sentence in his reading lessons.

2. Letter writing should be continued in this grade, and extended to include business letters, notes of invitation, acceptance, regret, etc.

"The chief requisites of a business letter are clearness, correctness. and conciseness." It should treat of business matters only, avoiding social or family topics that bear no relation to the subject matter of the correspondence. Brevity is desirable, but not at the expense of the correct construction of sentences. The omission of subject or verb should be avoided; also such abbreviations as "gents" for "gentlemen."

The following are appropriate forms for business letters :

LETTER OF INTRODUCTION.

Indianapolis, Ind.,
Feb. 1, 1877.

A. P. Stanton, Esq.,
Dublin, Ind.

Dear Sir,—Permit me to introduce to you the bearer, Mr. Charles C. Brown, who visits your city for the purpose of seeking employment as a civil engineer. He is a graduate of the Polytechnic Institute at Troy, New York, and is both honest and capable.

Any assistance that you may render him will be esteemed by me a personal favor.

Very truly yours,
John Smith.

MERCANTILE LETTER.

Richmond, Ind.,
March 22, 1877.

Messrs. Bowen, Stewart & Co.,
Indianapolis, Ind.

Gentlemen,—Please send to us by express, at your earliest convenience, the following:

4 doz. Hadley's Lessons in Language;
2 doz. copies Helen's Babies, paper;
3 doz. slates, 7x11.

When forwarded, please send invoice.

Very respectfully yours,
Jones & Son.

The following are appropriate forms for notes of invitation, acceptance, etc.:

NOTE OF INVITATION.

Mr. and Mrs. David Graham request the pleasure of Dr. and Mrs. Brown's company at dinner, on Wednesday, March 6th, at six o'clock.

An early answer is requested.

701 Meridian St.

NOTE OF ACCEPTANCE.

Dr. and Mrs. Brown accept with pleasure the kind invitation of Mr. and Mrs. Graham for Wednesday evening, March 6th.

608 Illinois St.

Monday, March 4th.

3. In the previous grades pupils have been frequently called upon to separate objects into their parts. In this grade they should be led to discover the different principles or bases upon which such separation may be made, and to name the parts upon each basis. The object of this exercise is to teach the fundamental principles of analysis. There are many bases upon which this separation may be made, but it is sufficient, for the present, to consider only two or three.

1. We may consider the *use, design,* or *office* of the parts: as, *the handle, the blade, the rivets, the back-spring, etc.*, of a pocket-knife; *the seat, the back, the top* or *table, the shelf, the legs, etc.*, of a school-desk; *the foundation, the walls, the roof, the windows, the doors, the rooms, the partitions, etc.*, of a house. This analysis may be carried another step, by separating each of these parts into subordinate parts, which, in turn, may be separated into other parts, until the analysis is complete. An exhaustive analysis is not required in this grade, but only so much as is necessary to give the pupil such practice in Division, as shall assist him in preparing an outline for the description of many classes of objects.

2. We may consider *material* as the basis of separation; in which case the parts of the knife are *iron, steel, brass, pearl* or *horn,* etc.; the parts of the school-desk are *wood, iron, paint,* or *varnish, putty, screws,* etc.

3. An object may be separated into parts on the basis of *relative position* of these parts: as, *top, bottom, inside, outside, corner, edge, back,* etc.

It often occurs that the same name is given to a part obtained upon two or more different principles of separation; as in the case of the screws of the desk. From one point of view they may be considered manufactured material, and from another, they may be considered as a part *used* to hold the other parts of the desk together.

Exercises, such as are indicated above, are of great value in training the child to think, which, as has been said, is one of the principal results sought in teaching composition.

4. Pursuing the line of thought suggested in the preceding paragraph, the pupil is next taught to classify the attributes of an object on the basis of the sense employed in gaining a knowledge of these attributes. Objects should be described by stating (1) the attributes known through the sense of sight; (2) those known through the sense of touch; (3) those known through the sense of hearing, of smell, of taste; (4) those known by experiment; as, *flexible, brittle, soluble,* etc.

Instruction upon the subjects suggested in this and the preceding paragraph, should be given in a conversational manner, the teacher relying chiefly upon oral drill to familiarize the pupil with the rules that are to guide him in making these different analyses.

Written exercises should occasionally be required to test the pupil's ability to do the work alone. In conducting these lessons, and all similar ones, the teacher should lead the pupils to observe the law of method, which requires that the parts or attributes upon any one basis shall all be given, before any of those upon another basis are mentioned.

5. The description of pictures, and the invention of stories suggested by them should be practiced as in the preceding grade. At least five exercises of this kind should be prepared during the year.

6. One re-production from memory of something read or told by the teacher, should be required each month.

7. Once each month, the pupils should be required to write an impromptu description of some object with which they are familiar.

8. Pupils in this grade, should be held for the proper use of capitals and marks of punctuation. (See Chapter X.)

9. Pupils should never be allowed to begin to write a composition, until they have prepared and written an outline of the theme in the order in which it is to be discussed. By obeying this direction through all the grades, the habit will be formed of carefully studying a subject before undertaking to instruct others in regard to it.

10. At least five selections of prose or poetry should be learned and recited during the year.

11. At least one impromptu exercise should be given each week, which may take the place of some other recitation, and be a written recitation, or a review of some topic in geography, natural science, etc.

CHAPTER VI.

Sixth Year Grade.—Grammar.

The course in the preceding grades has prepared the pupil to begin the study of technical grammar. In those grades, prominence has been given to collecting, arranging, and expressing thoughts; i. e., to composition. But if the teacher has done what the course suggests, the foundation has been laid for an intelligent study of the sentence as a whole, and in its parts. This study is so different from that of composition, that for the next three or four years, the two subjects must be taught separately. In this grade, three lessons each week should be given in grammar, and two, in composition. This plan will enable the teacher to carry on the two subjects at the same time, and apply the knowledge gained in one to instruction in the other.

The following suggests the course to be pursued in teaching

Grammar.

All necessary information in regard to the subject matter of these lessons will be found in "Lessons in Grammar," Part I. of this manual. It is only designed in this place to suggest the amount of work to be done in this grade, and to give some hints as to the method.

The teacher should first lead the pupil to form definitions of a *thought*, and a *sentence*.

The following is one method of doing this:

1. Request the pupils to think something of an object: as, *an apple*. Questions may be asked as follows:

"How many have thought something about this apple?" (Answer by raising hands.)

"How can I learn what you have thought?" *Ans.*—"We must tell you."

"What will you use to tell me?" *Ans.*—"Words."

"Where is the thought formed?" *Ans.*—"In our minds."

Teacher.—"Yes; but I can not know what your thought is until you have expressed it in some way. You might make up a certain kind of face, and then I should know that you thought the apple was sour; or you might point to something red, and then I should know that you thought the apple was red; and in these ways I would learn your thoughts. But the common way of expressing thoughts is by the use of words. Each one may now express the thought in his mind about this apple, in words. (Pupils answer by forming complete sentences.)

Teacher.—"When you thought sweetness, redness, hardness, etc., of the apple, you formed *a thought*; when you expressed these thoughts in words, you formed *a sentence.*"

1. A *sentence* is a group of words expressing a thought.

In some such way, as suggested above, the following statements and definitions should be developed:

2. Every *thought* has three elements, viz.: *the subject* of thought, *the predicate* of thought, and *the thinking* or *judging act*.

3. Every *sentence* has three elements, viz.: *the subject, the predicate,* and *the copula.*

NOTE.—1. Care should be taken to avoid confounding the subject of the thought with the subject of the sentence.

2. Numerous exercises should be given to illustrate each statement and definition. Original sentences should be required of pupils, illustrating the same, and enough practice given to make them familiar with every step taken.

4. Each element of the sentence may consist of one word, or two or more words: as, "Apples are ripe;" "The government of England, which is a limited monarchy, is strong and enduring."

5. When any element of a sentence consists of two or more words, it may generally be separated into a principal and a modifying part.

Exercise.

a. Numerous sentences should be selected, having one or more of the elements composed of a principal and a modifying part.

b. These sentences should be analyzed by naming (1) all the words composing each element; (2) the principal part of each element; (3) the modifying part of each element.

c. Pupils should be practiced in distinguishing modifyers as single words, phrases, and clauses.

NOTE.—In all the preceding exercises, the copula and predicate should be expressed by different words.

6. The copula and predicate are generally combined in one word: as, "John *writes.*"

NOTE.—Give numerous exercises illustrating this, and lead the pupil to see that these *attributive verbs* express both the *judging act* and the *predicate* of thought.

Exercise.

Analyze numerous sentences, in which the predicate and copula are united in one word, and one or more elements have modifying parts.

7. Sentences are divided into four classes, viz.: Declarative, Interrogative, Imperative, and Exclamatory.

A Declarative Sentence simply affirms the predicate of the subject.

An Interrogative Sentence asks a question.

An Imperative Sentence expresses a command.

An Exclamatary Sentence expresses strong feeling.

Exercise.

Pupils should select and write sentences under each of these classes, and analyze each.

Attributes.

8. Pupils should be led to discover the differences between qualities, actions, and conditions, and to see that they are *attributes* of objects and not *parts*.

Exercise.

a. Pupils should point out and classify the different words expressing attributes in selected sentences.

b. They should compose sentences in which the different kinds of attributes are expressed.

Parts of Speech.

9. Pupils should next be led to discover that words may be separated into classes on the basis of use: as, (1) words used to name objects, called *nouns*; (2) words used to name attributes of objects, called *adjectives*; (3) words used to name attributes of other attributes, called *adverbs*; (4) words used to denote objects without naming them, called *pronouns*; (5) words used to express the thinking or judging act of the mind, called *verbs*; (6) words used to show relation between objects, or between attributes and objects, called *prepositions*; (7) words used to show relation of thoughts, called *conjunctions*; (8) words used to express feeling, called *interjections*.

All the information that the teacher will need in regard to the matter to be taught, will be found in the chapters that treat upon these subjects in Part I.

All that is required of pupils in this grade, in regard to the parts of speech, is to learn the definition of each, and to be able to classify the words in their reading lessons, as determined by their use in expressing the thought.

CHAPTER VII.

Sixth Year Grade.—Composition.

1. Pupils in this grade should review all the rules for the formation of *plurals*, and the *possessive case*, learned in the preceding grades, and should learn the additional rules given on pages 46, 47, and 49, of "Lessons in Grammar."

2. At least one carefully prepared composition should be written each month. It is recommended that one of these be a description of something that it will be profitable for the pupils to study thoroughly, because of the valuable information acquired. Another may be a comparison between two cities; two nations; the manners and customs of two races of people; two classes of animals; or some similar theme. Subjects should be chosen with reference to some study pursued by the pupils. The work in natural science will suggest one or more themes: e. g., "Description of a spider;" "History of a frog;" and the like. At least one carefully prepared letter should be written.

3. Pupils should practice expressing the thoughts of a poem in prose. This may be done in connection with the lesson in reading. The poem should be carefully studied, the number of paragraphs determined, and the pupils encouraged to give a "free translation" of it in prose.

4. One imaginary sketch should be prepared. The subject may be, "A journey across the Continent;" "A visit to Paris;" "The home I would like to have;" "A storm at sea;" or any similar theme, about which information can be easily obtained.

5. The rules for punctuation and capitals should be carefully observed, and the pupils should be held for the correct spelling of all words. The free use of the dictionary should be encouraged in the preparation of compositions.

6. Impromptu exercises, as in other grades, should occasionally take the place of the regular recitation in one or more studies.

7. It is of the greatest importance that each subject be carefully and methodically studied under the direction of the teacher, before the pupil begins to write the composition that is to be presented as his final production.

Before the pupils begin to study a theme, the teacher should have prepared an outline, and have written a composition. She will thus know the lan of study that the pupils are to pursue, and will know how to help them in gaining information. Besides, she will know better the difficulties that the pupils will encounter, and, therefore, be more patient with those that fail. It is not necessary to wait each week until the hour arrives for the recitation in composition, before any reference is made to this work. When a subject is before the school for study, some reference should be made to it each day, in the recitation in grammar, or reading, or at some other time, and such help given as the pupils need.

CHAPTER VIII.

Seventh Year Grade.—Grammar.

1. Teachers are expected to pursue the same general method of instruction in this grade as in the preceding, and to teach the classification of the parts of speech, and of sentences, as presented in the first twelve chapters of "Lessons in Grammar."

The attempt should not be made to teach these chapters exhaustively, since the pupils will be required to go over the same work in the next grade.

The measure of the success of the teacher will be largely determined by the pupil's knowledge of the uses of these different classes of sentences, and parts of speech, in expressing thought. The pupil must always be led to see the necessity for each classification, before it is taught to him. The analysis of sentences is an important part of the work required. Before the pupil leaves this grade, he should be able to analyze most of the sentences in his reading lessons with ease.

Composition.

The rules and methods taught in the preceding grades are applicable to this. The teacher should study carefully the course prescribed for them.

2. The compositions in this grade should be more elaborate than those previously required, and themes should be chosen that will demand greater research. Sufficient time should, therefore, be given for the preparation of each composition. An average of one each month, is all that can be properly prepared.

The following themes are suggested: (1) a description of some historical picture, and the narration of the events suggested by it; (2) history of a block of coal; (3) a biography; (4) description of some city or building; (5) narration of the events related in some poem; (6) history of a dew-drop; (7) subject taken from the work in geography; (8) a subject taken from the work in history; (9) a social letter.

The following outline suggests one plan that may be followed in preparing a biography of Christopher Columbus:

1. Time and place of birth.
2. Opportunities for education.
3. Vocation in early life.
4. The popular opinion in regard to the shape of the earth at this time.
5. The opinion of Columbus.
6. How he proposed to prove the truth of his opinion.
7. His preparation for the enterprise.
8. His difficulties in procuring aid.
9. The like experience of Prof. Morse, the inventor of the electric telegraph.
10. The first voyage of Columbus.
11. The number of his voyages and the result of each.
12. The ungrateful conduct of the King of Spain.
13. His death in poverty, and pompous funeral.
14. The honor of naming the continent he had discovered conferred upon another.
15. Importance of his discoveries to Spain.
16. Character of Columbus.

3. Impromptu exercises should be required as in preceding grades.

An excellent way of preparing the reading lesson, is to require the pupils to write in their own language the thoughts expressed by the author.

4. Five or more selections of prose or poetry should be committed to memory and recited before the school. A portion of the time for the reading lesson may be taken occasionally for these recitations.

5. All errors in the pronunciation and use of words, and in the construction of sentences, should be corrected. The teachers in all the upper grades, are expected to know what has been taught in the grades below, and to see that the rules there learned are observed by the pupils in their schools.

CHAPTER IX.

Eighth Year Grade.

1. The "Lessons in Grammar" are to be completed by the pupils in this grade.

2. Ten compositions should be written during the year. The following themes are suggested.

DESCRIPTION.

"The City of Indianapolis;" "The Marion County Court House;" "The human eye."

NARRATION.

"Christopher Columbus;" "Roger Williams;" "Alexander Hamilton;" "Abraham Lincoln;" "The events that led to the Mexican war;" "The events that led to the Missouri Compromise;" "The events that led to the late Civil War;" "The process of digestion;" "Making glass."

COMPARISON AND CONTRAST.

"Washington and Lincoln;" "The first settlers of Virginia and those of Massachusetts;" "Webster and Calhoun."

DIVISION.

"The Constitution of the United States."

One social and one business letter should be written.

The following is suggested as an outline for a composition on "A comparison between the settlers of Massachusetts and those of Virginia."

1. Character of the early settlers of Massachusetts.
2. Motives for emigrating to America.
3. Character and motives of the early settlers of Virginia.
4. Compare the government and social condition of the two colonies.
5. State causes of this difference: (1) different objects of the colonists; (2) difference in the character of the people; (3) difference in climate and soil.
6. Compare the influence of the two colonies, in determining the present condition of the Nation.

3. Pupils should learn to recognize and define a simile, a metaphor, a personification, an allegory, and a comparison. This instruction should be given in connection with the lessons in reading.

4. Pupils in this grade should be able to point out the principal and modifying elements of any sentence in the reading lessons, at sight.

5. The rules for capitals, punctuation, and spelling, should be carefully observed.

6. The teacher is referred to the course of the preceding grades, for suggestions as to the methods to be pursued in teaching this subject.

7. Pupils should be required to learn two or more selections of standard poetry.

8. There should be four lessons each week in grammar, two in composition, and four in reading, throughout the year.

CHAPTER X.

Rules for Punctuation.

Rule I.—A *Period* should be placed after every declarative and every imperative sentence, and after every abbreviation.

Rule II.—A *Colon*, a *Semi-colon*, or a *Comma* may be used before a direct quotation.

Rule III.—A *Colon* is used after a member of a sentence that is complete in itself, but is immediately followed by some remark, or explanation; as, "To reason with him was vain: he was too angry."

Rule IV.—The *Colon* is placed between members of a sentence that are sub-divided by a semi-colon.

Rule V.—The *Semi-colon* is placed between parts that are subdivided by the comma.

Rule VI.—The *Comma* is used after each word in a succession of particulars; as, "Earth, air, and water teem with life."

NOTE.—When there are but two particulars connected by a conjunction, no comma is used.

Rule VII.—The *Comma* is used to set off interposed words and phrases, and the foreign element in a complex sentence; as, "John, come here;" "This, we think, is true;" "This, however, is not my purpose."

Rule VIII.—The *Comma* may be inserted to avoid ambiguity; as, "He who teaches, often learns much."

Rule IX.—The *Exclamation Point* is used to denote intense feeling; as, "Oh me! that awful dream!

Rule X.—The *Interrogation Point* is used to denote a question.

Rule XI.—The *Dash* is used to denote an abrupt suspension or turn in the thought; as, "Is it possible—but I will not ask the question."

Rule XII.—*Quotation marks* are used to set off a direct quotation; as, Socrates said, "I believe the soul is immortal."

www.ingramcontent.com/pod-product-compliance
Lightning Source LLC
Chambersburg PA
CBHW020153170426
43199CB00010B/1018